MELFORD MEMORIES

Ernest Ambrose in uniform
From print owned by Ian Sandham

MELFORD MEMORIES

RECOLLECTIONS OF 94 YEARS

ERNEST AMBROSE

 EYE BOOKS
NON-FICTION

Published by Eye Books
29A Barrow Street
Much Wenlock
Shropshire
TF13 6EN

www.eye-books.com

Originally published 1972
This edition published in 2022 by the Long Melford Historical &
Archaeological Society, with funding from the Thomas Howlett Fund and
the Long Melford Heritage Trust.

Cover design by Nell Wood
Typeset in Adobe Garamond Pro, Bodoni URW Regular and IM FELL
Double Pica

British Library Cataloguing in Publication Data
A catalogue record for this book is available from the British Library

ISBN 9781785633683

Front cover picture: Hall Street, Long Melford, 1904, from postcard owned
by Keith Slater
Back cover pictures: Ernest Ambrose in uniform; Ernest Ambrose's first
wedding, taken at the back of Cocoanut House, Long Melford, from prints
owned by Ian Sandham

Contents

References to places or businesses as they are now refer to 1972, when the book was originally published.

Foreword

I vividly recall the impact that this wonderful book made when it was first published in 1972.

Melford Memories records the fascinating recollections of one man, Ernest Ambrose, who lived in the village for over ninety-four years.

Beginning with his schooldays in the 1880s, he recalls a very different Long Melford – when the Green was grazed by sheep and hosted a horse fair. He remembers elephants (from the circus) and dancing bears being seen in the streets. He describes the dragoons quelling the riot of 1885, while including numerous other stories – some amusing, some sad – about life in those times. It is an illuminating account of local interest, but also has a much wider historical value.

I am thrilled that the village's Historical and Archaeological Society, together with the Long Melford Heritage Trust, have now enabled this redesigned fiftieth anniversary edition to be published.

It brings Ernest's village to life again for another generation to treasure and enjoy.

Ashley Cooper
President of the Long Melford Historical and Archaeological Society
October 2022

PREFACE

From Sir Richard W. Hyde Parker, Bart.
President of the Long Melford Historical and Archaeological
Society

It is with great pleasure and honour that I recommend these recollections of Ernest Ambrose, so well described by his wife.

Here is a true picture of the life and times of one man, spanning ninety-four years. Many of us who read this book will find the great changes which have taken place during these years incredible, and others will find their memories sharpened.

We are then left with the familiar questions. Were the good old days good? Is today good? What qualities have we lost or gained? Is it not essential that we ponder these questions, standing as we do today, often wavering, as we try to shape our future?

Richard Hyde Parker (1937-2022)
Melford Hall
September 1972

INTRODUCTION

My husband has always been fond of telling stories. He relates incidents which occurred in his youth ninety years ago as vividly as though they were recent events. One day the idea came to me: why not write down some of these tales and present them in the form of memoirs, and so preserve a record of days gone by. I have endeavoured to do this as conscientiously as possible, at the same time doing my best to avoid giving offence to living relatives.

I hope our little effort will serve to present a faithful picture of what life was like in a quiet corner of Suffolk before it was overtaken by the technological advances of the present day.

I would like to record our thanks to Sir Richard W. Hyde Parker, Bart., President of the Long Melford Historical and Archaeological Society, for allowing us to include a photograph of a portrait from his Melford Hall collection. Our thanks too, to Thomas H. Howlett, Esq., Secretary of the Society, for his encouragement and the very valuable help he has given in collecting and preparing the photographs, assisted by R. Burn, Esq. Also our appreciation to R. Wickham Partridge, Esq. for his help with publishing.

Emily Rebecca Ambrose
Sudbury, Suffolk
September 1972

ILLUSTRATIONS

Schooldays in the 1800s

I wondered why Ma got me up so early. I usually had to stay in bed till Pa had gone to work; but on this special day I was told to get dressed in my best clothes. My face was scrubbed at the kitchen pump, my boots were smeared with blacking, and I was hustled along to have breakfast with Father. "You're going to school today," said Ma. "You're three now and it's high time you started. You can go down with Pa on his way to work." So that was the meaning of all the fuss. Pushing my floppy cap well over my head and ears as well, and giving me a quick kiss as if of apology, Ma sent me off to school.

We lived in a cottage in Church Row, so the journey was not a long one. We walked down the road to the Black Lion and crossed over where the roads from Cambridge, Bury and Sudbury converge. At the top of the Green was a busy old-fashioned shop presided over by Mr. John Spilling and his family. He was already out there sweeping the cobbled forecourt. "Mornin' Mr. Spilling," said Pa. "Mornin' John." I was bursting to tell him I was going to school, but even at my tender age I had already learnt that small boys must not speak until spoken to, so I held my peace.

Opposite Mr. Spilling's Old Top Shop on the corner of the

Green were two remaining plinths of the old market cross, which had been destroyed during the Commonwealth. I loved to sit on these thick stones and watch the horses and carts and carriages go by and see all the interesting people on the road as well as the cattle and other animals grazing on the Green. This morning there was only a little donkey tethered to a post and a drover with a herd of cows grazing. Pa went on steadily down the casey (causeway) alongside the Green and I perforce had to run a little now and then to keep up with him.

We soon arrived at the village school and I was thrust inside without much ceremony. Pa produced the one penny for a week's education and I was duly established in our local seat of learning.

Memories of my first day at school are somewhat dim, but as it is now ninety-one years ago perhaps I may be forgiven. However I do remember my teacher, Miss Syborn. She was very kind and gentle to me, as I was a new boy I suppose. She squeezed me in on the front bench, telling the other children not to push me. She seemed very big and stately, but this was probably accentuated by the fact that she wore a long black dress which swept the floor and rustled a great deal, and a stiff high-necked blouse with lots of ruffles about it. Her hair was piled up high and finally came to a point, and I spent much time wondering however she managed to keep it that way. As I was a small boy for my age she seemed to tower above me from a great height, and I looked up to her with awe and respect. She had a bustle which stuck out at the back and some of the boldest pupils would dare one another to tiptoe behind her and gently place a slate pencil on this protuberance. I thought this a very bold act!

I was very happy at school as I knew quite a lot of the

children, especially those who came from my end of the village. The school windows were high so our attention was not distracted. The brick walls were all decorated with educational and scriptural texts and pictures. The blackboard was the chief aid to learning, combined with the constant repetition at the top of our voices of the Creed and Catechism, the Ten Commandments and scriptural texts, the alphabet and multiplication tables.

It was a church school and the rector, the Rev. Martyn, or one of his two curates, visited the school every Friday to give us lessons on the Bible and hear us recite our texts. Religious knowledge, strict obedience and the three Rs were the foundation of our learning, in that order, followed when we were older by history, geography and nature study. The continuous chanting of so many facts was a hopeless mumbo-jumbo to me at first, but gradually light dawned and I began to see what it was all about and enjoyed finding out more.

The chief aim seemed to be to give children sufficient education to carry on the life of the village, which was at that time a self-contained unit. Very few ventured outside the parish boundaries to earn a living in those early days. They mostly stayed in their own neighbourhood and started work as soon as they could, to add to the family's slender exchequer. The school authorities were not too strict about attendance and if any child was wanted to work in the fields during the week they didn't make much fuss so long as the penny was paid every Monday morning. This charge was later raised to twopence and later still to fourpence.

Discipline was stern when I was a boy and the cane was used somewhat freely. Quite small children were made to stand in the corner facing the wall for some slight misdemeanour; the girls having to put their pinnies over their heads and the boys "hands on head". In the Big Boys the more unruly ones (or those whose sums wouldn't go right) had to stand in the corner holding a pile of slates on their head.

Our head master, Mr. J. Phillips, was a learned man and a very good teacher. Though he was a strict disciplinarian we all liked and respected him. We felt we could always rely on him being fair. If we did wrong we knew we would be punished and we accepted this as just; and in this matter he always had the backing of our parents. We were brought up to respect (or honour was the word usually used) God, our parents, our teachers and especially the two squires of the village and the rector, who were the appointed leaders of our little community.

There was a comfortable family feeling about our school, and the village too. We felt we all belonged to one another. We all knew each other and the teachers lived in close proximity to our homes, so they had good knowledge of our home life and family background. The strong moral teachings instilled in us produced a firm foundation and a clear understanding of right and wrong, and in consequence the school was remarkably free from dishonesty both in word and deed, and swearing was never allowed. The only time I had a whack on the hand from teacher's cane was when a prim little girl in a stiff white pinny decorated with an abundance of goffered frills (a sure sign of opulence) and with a lot of bobbing ringlets, dared me to say a swear word to her. I promptly said Damn! Then she told teacher I had sworn at her. For a long time after that I hated little girls, especially those with ringlets; but I never swore again – at least not in school!

I saw this same little girl in the Top Shop a few days later, jam jar in hand, asking for "a pen'oth a golden syrip which poor people calls trickle". When I told Ma about it she said, "The stuck up bit of a mawther."

Boys and girls were segregated from an early age, and certainly after the age of seven, when we went up into the Big Boys or Big Girls. But even as infants we usually sat in our own groups except for needlework when the girls had to sew long seams of tiny stitches and the boys had to knit. I can still recall my feeble efforts at this art. The girls were instructed to cast on and do a few rows of knitting for the boys. You could very easily see where the girls left off and the boys took over, and mine was no exception! But I did excel at one subject at school and that was music. We had singing lessons with tonic sol fa, and this came easily to me. I suddenly felt I had music inside me which wanted to come out and I revelled in it.

As we got older we were allowed to use slates and pencils. The agonising squeaks these produced made me squirm. I can't imagine what it must have meant to teacher. When we went up into the Big Boys we were allowed to use pen and ink. For this purpose we had copy books, which were precious as they were in short supply. In them were printed in copperplate writing various proverbs which we had to reproduce in similar copperplate style. I can still remember my laborious efforts in those early days, and still remember many of the proverbs:

Do not grasp too much or you may lose all.
Waste not, want not.
Look before you leap.
The wise man looking at the stars fell into a ditch.

I always thought the last one very funny. But as a result of our laborious and much repeated efforts to write "proper" these

5

precepts became firmly fixed in our minds. They all seemed very good sense to me.

We had plenty of reading and spelling lessons and were taught very thoroughly to read and pronounce words correctly, but once we got outside we lapsed immediately into our own native dialect, and most of our h's were dropped on the school doorstep. We almost spoke two different languages.

Among the villagers at that time speech was slovenly and lazy. There was so much illiteracy that folk didn't know how words were spelt, or if they did they were too lazy to pronounce them properly. Their vocabulary, often spattered with mispronounced Biblical quotations, was slow and ponderous, as often happens to people who live in small or isolated communities. It was far easier to say "Thass-wa-a allus-saay" than to enunciate clearly "That is what I always say". It rolls smoothly off the tongue and there is something very pleasant about the sound.

Those in authority, however, did their best to improve education among the older folk in the village, and they organised little gatherings of people to hear Penny Readings. These were held in our school in the evenings and were conducted usually by one of the Rev. Martyn's charming daughters. A selection from Dickens' works was the most popular reading and the meeting would be concluded by an extract from a "good book" of an edifying nature.

My grandmother used to go to these Penny Readings and would call on Mother on her way home to tell her about them, and laugh and talk about the people there, retailing the latest bits of village gossip over a dish of tea. Sometimes these readings would be held at the rectory in the parish room and a full house was always guaranteed on these occasions, as a cup of tea and a biscuit would be thrown in.

2

MY HOME AND FAMILY

When we were quite small we lived in a cosy little cottage near the rectory. It was one of four cottages which, in the Middle Ages, was the tithe barn belonging to the church, and later converted. A lot of farm workers lived at our end of the village, and if you looked out of the window about five thirty in the morning you would see them on their way to work with a couple of stone jars of home-made beer slung over their shoulders.

My parents were of yeoman stock, steady and moderate in their way of life. My mother was a careful manager and a good cook and could make a lovely meal out of very little. We weren't what you would call poor, but if any of us lost a shilling it was a disaster. We lived simply, without any luxuries; we weren't allowed much sugar, that was too dear.

Father always kept a pig or two in the garden and so we usually had a supply of ham and pork. He even had enough to sell some to neighbours or friends occasionally. A specially nice ham was always reserved for Christmas, and how delicious it was! The hams were cured in big tubs in the kitchen, and I often had to baste them by pouring over them black treacle, old beer (must be old) and coarse dark brown sugar. After a few weeks of this treatment they were sent to Bixby's bakehouse across the

Green to smoke. Sometimes legs of pork were pickled in brine and water. These were lovely too!

Pa also kept ducks and some bantam hens. The ducks were very amusing. We used to hatch the ducklings in the back garden. When they were old enough we would drive the mother duck across the top green to Clappits pond by Little Holland and the ducklings would all follow her. At five o'clock without fail every evening one of us would go across and fetch the ducks and their families home for the night. This went on for three or four days or so, after which the old ducks would lead their own families back home by themselves, and didn't wait for us to collect them. Neighbours would say, "There goo owld John's ducks. Must be tea time."

My mother was a Norfolk woman and came from a little village not far from Sandringham. She knew the future Queen Alexandra and often had a chat with her. The Queen was fond of visiting the village and enjoyed talking with the village women about their families and her own and comparing notes. She was obviously very much at home with them.

Mother had lots of friends in Melford. Indeed we all did as we all knew one another (and one another's business too). One of Ma's special friends was the housekeeper at Melford Hall. She was a very important person in her own right and held sway over all the other indoor servants. She had her own quarters at the Hall and Ma would sometimes visit her there in her own private sitting room. On occasion Mother would take me with her and I was overawed by the splendour of the occasion, even though we only went in by the tradesmen's entrance. How important I felt when we were escorted up the back stairs by a maid dressed in smart black uniform with a trim white apron and cap with long ribbons hanging down her

Melford Hall, c. 1840. Drawing by S. Clarke of Long Melford.
Note the man with the fowling piece standing near the Hall.
From print owned by Mrs. Howe

back, who bobbed to the housekeeper and announced us as though we were of importance.

I remember the housekeeper, big and tall but much fatter than teacher, with a chatelaine attached to her broad belt, from which dangled all sorts of keys, pencil, scissors etc. How important it made her look. I wouldn't have liked to have got into her bad books.

I still remember the big bowl of fruit on a table covered by a rich velvet cloth. There were fruits I had never seen before such as pineapple, figs, peaches and grapes, many of which were grown in the big greenhouse in the grounds. I also saw tomatoes there for the first time. I believe they were being used as a table decoration. At first they were thought unfit to eat. It was all very exciting for a small boy. Sometimes I was given an orange, of which there were very few about at that time. We used to eat peel and all! Mother used to enjoy her visits too, but she was more interested in the latest local gossip and in the excellent dripping which she could buy for twopence a pound.

As well as the big greenhouse there were fish ponds or "stews" in the grounds where in the old days they could get a fresh supply of fish at any time. They also had a pigeon or dove cote, called by the locals a "duffus", which provided food for the family. A few local fishermen had permission to fish in the Hall ponds and I remember Bob Sewell telling me he had taken some very fine pike from Melford Hall ponds, weighing up to seven pounds. But there were larger fish still in Kentwell Moat. They had carp weighing up to thirty pounds.

I used to think how lovely it would be to work at Melford Hall. Everything was so splendid and the servants seemed to be fine, upstanding, important sort of people. They all had their proper status and had to be treated with respect according to their position. They had fine uniforms too, provided for them, and lived in a way I thought was grand style not far short of the squire himself and his family, who all seemed to me to be very kind and generous towards their employees.

If a boy on leaving school was lucky enough to get a job as a back'us boy at one of these halls he was considered to be very fortunate indeed, this being the first rung of the ladder to success in life. He was exhorted by his parents and elders to be sure to work hard, be strictly honest and behave yourself, and "do as yer telled bor".

My father's mother lived near us in Church Row and I spent a lot of time with her. She remembered the time when there were deer in the Melford Hall park, and she was fond of telling me about the great shooting parties and magnificent hunt balls that were held in her young days. In Grandma's cottage (which was thatched) there was a big open fireplace and on each side were cupboards on the doors of which were carvings of the heads of Nell Gwyn and King Charles II. These were evidently very well done and one day her landlord, no doubt with an eye to their value, asked her to sell them to him. Grandma was very fond of these carvings and refused to part with them for some time. He became very insistent and in the end she relented, and he gave her the princely sum of two shillings and sixpence each for them.

In her young days Grandma was with a family who spent some time each summer at Carisbrook Castle on the Isle of Wight. She used to tell me about the splendours of the castle (as well as some of the problems of the servants' lives there) and also of how she would occasionally see Queen Victoria, on one of her visits to the castle, out driving in her low carriage escorted by her faithful friend John Brown.

Grandma must have had quite an exciting life when she was young. She had travelled quite a lot by stagecoach, and had been to Astley's Royal Circus and to Vauxhall Gardens pleasure grounds in London.

Grandma was a strong character, very hard-working, very blunt and full of fight. She was always very kind to me. I think perhaps I was a favourite of hers. She always wore a long black dress (nearly everyone seemed to wear black in those days) and of course buttoned boots. On Sundays she put on a pretty lacy white cap and a lacy tippett to smarten up her dress.

She was an adept at using her old tinder box and could quickly get a light to her fires with flint and steel and paraffin rag, though of course matches had by now become popular. Brimstone matches were the first I remember. They smelt and spluttered and sizzled and didn't always function very well.

11

Later on they brought in "safety" ones, from which sparks would fly! Grandma always used the old Russian tallow candles, slow burning and smelly.

Grandpa, who was a brewer by trade and brewed beer for local pubs, died at an early age and Grandma became a widow when she was only forty. In those days there was no such thing as a widow's pension, so she was obliged to find some means of supporting herself. She took in laundry from the rectory, and every Monday morning one of the many servants brought her a big linen basket piled high with clothes. By the time I was ready to go to school the little cottage would be filled with steam and a strong smell of yellow soap and the linen would be boiling away in the copper in the wash'us attached to the house. I always had a private hope that Mondays would be a fine day, and that if by any chance it turned out wet the clothesline wouldn't break when laden with washing. Grandma would always be so pleased if the clothes got nicely hazelled, just ready for the next process.

When I got home from school in the afternoon I was usually in time to help with the mangling. The mangle was a giant machine taking up one whole wall of the little kitchen. It consisted of a huge trough filled with heavy flints with three big rollers underneath. It made a tremendous noise as it clattered round. It took all my childhood's strength to turn those giant wheels, but it was fine exercise. One day the index finger of my left hand got caught and I have been minus the top down to the first joint ever since.

After the mangling came the ironing and goffering and folding and airing. It was quite a prolonged work of art before the linen was ready to be stacked once again in the basket ready to go back to the rectory.

To augment her income further Grandma sold the very fine apples and pears which grew in her large garden, at the rate of twelve a penny. Later on she boarded children from Dr. Barnardo's Homes. Quite a number of families in the village offered hospitality to these children.

Grandma was a good living woman and very religious. The nearest she ever got to swearing was "Tarnation!" or "Confound it!", popular expressions at that time. She attended church regularly and took me with her while I was still quite small. At that period one had to get there early to get a seat, and everyone had their own favourite seats. Grandma's was in the south aisle. She would find the places in the prayer book for me and encourage my small efforts to join in the service.

The sermons were long and boring, but Grandma didn't appear to mind, and she would let me fall asleep on her shoulder at this stage. When she was young the sermons were far longer, sometimes up to an hour and a half. She remembered an old sexton named Wicks who had a long pole like a fishing rod. He would walk up and down the church during the sermon and if he found anyone fast asleep he would tap them on the head with his rod.

The singing of the choir and the beautiful organ music gripped me tremendously and its sound would still be ringing in my ears when I got home. One night I had a very vivid dream. I was sitting at the great organ and though I was so tiny, wonderful music was coming out of the huge instrument. I couldn't reach the pedals or the stops, but somehow or other I was able to play it because standing beside me was my father. It was a wonderful dream and I was enjoying it so much. I felt sad and disappointed to wake up and find it was only a dream.

3

ROADS AND TRAVELLERS: ITINERANT TRADERS AND ENTERTAINERS

When I was a small boy our roads were rough and uneven, with big flints and potholes, very dusty in summer and muddy with large pools of water in winter. Even the main roads were bad, the Bury road being one of the worst. From time to time they were made up with loads of stones. Old men and women were paid twopence a bushel for stone picking from farmers' fields, and small children were given a halfpenny, and these were used for the roads.

Our chief means of transport was still by foot, on horseback or by horse-drawn vehicles of various kinds. Journeys were often fraught with some danger and a trip to a neighbouring town or village was still something of an adventure.

I always got great pleasure sitting on the old step of the market cross at the top of the Green watching the people and animals passing along the roads. A common sight would be a flock of sheep and their shepherd with his hooked crook leading them. This was a Suffolk custom as well as a scriptural one. A well-trained dog would bring up the rear and keep the flock together. They would always stop on the Green for an hour or two for the sheep and shepherd to have a rest. The sheep would nibble contentedly at the grass and keep the Green in good order by spreading manure at the same time.

At other times we would see geese or ducks, pigs or cows, sometimes a hundred or more, being driven to market at Bury or Sudbury. At Christmas time especially, droves of turkeys and geese from Norfolk came through Melford. The drovers would tar the soles of their heavy boots to make them more comfortable for constant walking on the rough roads.

Later on the smaller animals would be brought in carts. There were almost always a few horses on the Green as it was used as a training ground for breaking in young animals. We boys would collect their droppings, which was beautiful stuff for the gardens. The villagers also used the Green for feeding their own animals, so it was always a busy place and interesting for us children.

As well as the animals there were all kinds of travellers on the roads. Fine men and sometimes women too on horseback. I used to sit and wonder where they all came from and where they were going to, and wonder too if one day I would be rich enough to have a lovely horse to go riding on. There were the smart carriages of the gentry, sometimes with two or perhaps four horses and splendid important-looking coachmen with cockaded hats, flourishing their whips with bows of ribbon tied on them, sitting high up on top of the box, and a footman at the back trying to look equally important, though we all knew quite well that he was really a much lesser light.

There were gentry too of lower estate. They often had broughams or smaller and less ornate carriages and no footman. There were farmers and tradesmen in their gigs or buggies, driving themselves with much flourishing of their whips and calling out jovially to friends in passing. Then perhaps single ladies, very genteel and modest in a small carriage, perhaps being driven by a manservant if they could afford one, trying to look as important as they could under their reduced circumstances.

Everyone had their appointed place in society in those days and though many tried hard to aspire to greater heights and ape the gentry, we all knew in which state we belonged – and other people too. We learnt this lesson early in life and accepted it. We had respect for those in authority above us, but nevertheless we maintained our own sturdy independence.

There were always many foot travellers of course and many gypsies in their brightly coloured vans, often quite a convoy of them, bringing up the rear with a donkey or pony. And always many tramps and beggars. I used to get quite excited about all the people and happenings I saw and would run home and tell Ma. Occasionally I would see the lord of the manor or the rector, and would dash home at once to report this happening. She would say, "I hope you raised your cap," and I would reply in the affirmative. They would sometimes even speak to me. That was really great!

I still remember the first day I encountered a dancing bear. I was quite used to seeing big animals like cows or horses, but this great creature frightened me out of my wits. Fortunately I was with Pa and hid behind his bulky form while I watched an incredible performance. The poor old bear, a big brown one, was shaggy and forlorn looking, and the man in charge, who had him on a long chain, looked even more doleful. They stopped outside the Black Lion and when the man sang a little lilting song and jigged up and down the great old bear reared up on its hind legs and shuffled about without much enthusiasm. Then the heavy pole which the man carried was tossed to the bear who caught it neatly across its two front paws and "danced" with it.

A few people gathered around to watch and applaud in a half-hearted manner, then dropped a few half pence in the old man's hat. Then to my astonishment both the man and the bear ambled into the back yard of the Lion, I learnt that they were both going to stay there for the night, the bear being boarded in one of the stables.

I could hardly sleep that night for worrying about that bear. Our back garden joined the stables of the Lion and in my dreams the great creature was either coming up our stairs or climbing in my bedroom window. I was out early the next morning to find out what was going to happen next, and was more than relieved to see them both wandering off along the Bury road.

Later on I saw quite a few of these dancing bears. Some were lovely, well-groomed creatures. Sometimes two or even more men, often Italians, had them. Gradually however this form of entertainment died out.

We often had visits from men and women with barrel organs, or street pianos, their owners monotonously turning the handle and churning out all sorts of music and popular songs. They were usually accompanied by a little monkey, dressed in some fancy costume, sitting on the top of the organ. Sometimes he would be put down on the road to carry the cup for the collection.

We had German string bands too, consisting of twelve or fourteen players. They must have walked miles from one place to another. I never saw any conveyance. These men were always very polite, and they played well – popular music from Strauss, Offenbach and Gilbert and Sullivan. I enjoyed listening to these bands and would stand and memorise the music and run home and try to play it on father's small organ.

On one occasion the bandsmen formed a little circle near the Black Lion and struck up some tune, when my little black and tan terrier wriggled his way into the centre, stuck his nose up in the air and howled protestingly. Woo...oo...oo. The few onlookers were delighted and I'm pretty sure the collection was slightly higher than usual. I believe these bands were occasionally hired for parties and so on.

Small parties of actors used to visit the village from time to time. They would often hire the Lecture Hall (now Working Men's Club) and put on a programme. Some of their shows were poor, but often they were very good and it was always good fun to attend their performances; you couldn't grumble at sixpence a time for the best seats. They would put on excerpts from Shakespeare plays; tragedies were always popular, especially *Murder in the Red Barn*. A vigorous and continuous amount of audience participation was expected and received. It was great fun.

We sometimes had visits from travelling theatres; a particular one I remember was named Waites. They came with horses and vans and brought all their own equipment, including stage and props, and would erect it on Smalley meadows. They too were well patronised and very popular.

We also had the travelling menagerie run by Bostock and Wombwell. They travelled all over England in great horse-drawn vans. They had a right to stand in the street (but not on the Green) and would erect their show in front of the houses (almost on their doorsteps) just beyond the Bull in Hall Street. They usually had among their collections one or two elephants, some monkeys, and a lion and tiger, often in cramped cages. I was sorry for the poor animals.

If some of the animals started roaring it could be heard right down the street and caused great excitement, especially among the small fry. A few of us boys looking round outside started to feed one of the elephants as he pushed his trunk beneath the cage, when one of them gave him some stones. The old elephant withdrew and shuffled and grunted, then out came his trunk again. The same boy bent down and got a horrible shower of stones right in his face. He had to run home quickly, having sustained some nasty injuries.

As well as all these travelling entertainers we had a lot of people walking or driving through the village offering all sorts of things for sale. There was the bag man, much loved by women, as in his voluminous canvas bag he carried a variety of small things such as ribbons and laces, cottons and dainty frilly things which ladies liked to use. Then there was the tea man, who called regularly every Monday morning. He was a little old man with a billy-goat beard, and he had a little pony and equally little canvas-covered van with home-made shutters. He sold only tea, wrapped in quarters of a pound, in cone-shaped bags. He had two varieties and mother always bought a quarter for sixpence; this lasted us for about a week. Some people used the leaves several times.

There was a jolly little man who called regularly with a pony and cart piled high with apples. He was a real character. He had a pleasant tenor voice and sang his wares, making up a little tune as he went along. Everyone called him Apple-O. "Come and buy my apples-O; pretty little apples-O." When anyone spoke to him he would sing his reply. He made a habit of walking up one side of the broad street and down the other side. One day he was near the chemist's shop when a woman near the Bull opposite thought he was going on over the bridge and called out to him. He promptly sang back to her "I go up this way; I come down that way. You must stop till I get there."

Another well-known character was a man, almost a dwarf, who had a wooden leg. He made a living of sorts by selling newspapers between Sudbury and Melford, the paper in most demand being the *Suffolk Free Press*, price twopence. But as papers in those day were shared among many people, I don't suppose he made much of a fortune. He had a donkey cart and his wooden leg stuck out in front, the cart was so small.

The Sand man was another regular caller. He did quite a good trade selling fine silver sand which he got from some local gravel pit. Villagers used to buy this sand to spread over their rough earth or brick floors. Some put down reeds or straw, and these could easily be replaced from time to time. Many couldn't afford the luxury of mats. The Sand man was a cheerful individual and he too used to advertise by singing out his wares. "Sand-O, one penny skip Sand-O."

Practical joking was a popular pastime and one day someone made up a parcel of dry horse manure and placed it in his path. Several kindred spirits stood round, hands in pockets, to see the fun. The Sand man stopped in his walk, picked up the parcel and sang "Hello, what's this?" He felt it carefully. "Baccy I hope." Then pressed it again. "Sugar I think." Then he opened it. "Turd be damned." He flung it down, but taking no offence he laughed and went on singing and calling out "Sand-O."

We also had the Egg man – twenty-four for a shilling – and the Muffin man carrying a tray of these dainties on his head and ringing a bell to announce his presence. Sometimes someone would come along selling chitterlings or hot rolls, two for a penny. There was the gypsy girl singing rather sweetly with her little bunches of lavender; the Hokey Pokey man and the one with ice cream lollipops, a penny a lump – a rather doubtful commodity.

The sweep would stroll along the street offering his services, pushing his supply of long brushes on a home-made barrow. Then there was the rag-and-bone man "any ole rag an bone, rab skin, rab bone". Toy windmills were offered in exchange so children eagerly sought something for this old man.

All sorts of things were sold on the streets when I was a boy: apples, pears, ripe strawberries, coal, paraffin, and of course *Old Moore's Almanack*, only a halfpenny. No home should be without one of those!

Sundays in particular brought a good crop of itinerant traders. Enterprising local men would order boxes, of fish from Lowestoft, which would be sent to Melford Station by early train. They would meet these consignments with a variety of barrows and little carts and donkeys, and walk up the long Melford street shouting out such things as winkles-O twopence a pint; fresh mackerels, kippers, bloaters, mussels, sprats, herrings etc. The women would come out of their cottages with plates and basins, and pick and choose their fish dainties for Sunday tea.

Another Sunday afternoon visitor was an old man (they always seemed to me to be old!) who used to collect watercress in the river and wander up the street shouting, "Water cress all fresh. Ha'penny a handful."

I mustn't forget to mention the bedraggled old tramp who would come up the road on Sundays, usually at dinner time, looking desperately miserable and dolefully singing "Abide with me". Sometimes in even more despondent mood we would hear "What will become of England if things go on this way". I took this seriously as a child and worried myself no end about it.

On Sweeps' Day, which was celebrated on May Day, a little party of men would come through the village dancing and singing. There would be one or two chimney sweeps carrying their long brushes, accompanied by a man playing the accordion, and another man dressed in a thick carpet with a hole in it for his head. They sang and danced up the street and collected money for "charity" (or for themselves).

Once a week on Thursday afternoons, a little one-horse bus would run from the Lion to Sudbury market. Just after dinner it would come up to the Lion and wait there for passengers to climb in and we children would stand and stare and admire. It was a smart little bus, well-kept, with a bright yellow roof. The driver sat outside on the box. The horse always had smart harness and trappings, which was not surprising as it belonged to Fred Neave the saddlemaker, who had a shop in Hall Street which later became Purdy's cafe. He was a nice man, a very good bass singer.

Grandma used his bus occasionally and as a special treat she would take me. The vehicle held six adults and any number of small children, and the journey cost sixpence.

4

Tradesmen, Craftsmen, Industries

When I was a boy there were several small shops at our end of the village. In the cottage next door lived Crowther Ambrose and his wife (no relation to us) and they used to make sausages. They bought best-quality pork and made these sausages in their kitchen. We often went in and watched them. They were delicious and the couple had a very good business, people coming from quite a distance to buy them.

Nearby was a sweet shop in one of the thatched cottages with a bow window. I liked to patronise this shop whenever I had any money, which by the way I had to work for by collecting firewood, chopping logs or running errands. One day I went to this shop and asked for a "farden's worth of licorice and can I have it in a paper please?" The rather stern-faced lady owner glared at me and said, "Do you want all the profit, boy?" It took me some time to find out what profit meant.

At the side of the Scutchers Arms in Westgate Street was a bakery run by Mr. Bixby, and at a small cottage nearby an old lady ran a library charging a farthing a week per book. On the opposite side of the road was a whitesmith named Downs. A blacksmith named Henry Sparrow had a forge nearby, and there was plenty of business for both these men.

Of course the Top Shop on the corner opposite the Black Lion was our biggest emporium. This shop was noted for its fine variety of delicious cheeses, which were stored and matured in their extensive cellars. One could sample several cheeses before deciding which to buy, at about threepence or fourpence a pound. They sold everything at this shop, from oil to groceries, from boots to hardware, clothes and medicines. It was a great place for the women to meet and catch up with the latest gossip.

One day one of the residents from the Hospital came in (we children called them the Spittle men). He sat down on a chair to wait. Seeing no other customers in the shop he had a look round and noticed a pile of butter on the counter, cut into quarters and unwrapped as was their practice at that time. It looked tempting and he couldn't resist. He picked one up, lifted his top hat, and popping the butter on his bald head, replaced his hat.

Now the grocer working at the back of the shop had a tiny spy hole in one of his shelves through which he could peer and observe when customers came in. And he saw what the Spittle man did. He came forward, greeted his customer cordially and served him. Then he said, "It's a cold mornin' Master 'ardy, come and have a drop a whisky in the back parlour."

"No, no, I marn't stop now. Thank 'ee all the same. I'll bid you good mornin'."

"Do you come, Master 'ardy. Come and git warm afore you goo."

And he was so persistent that he finally got the Hospital man into his back parlour, placed him in a chair before a roaring fire and gave him a glass of whisky. The poor man got hotter and hotter and was soon mopping his brow while butter poured down his face.

"Don't bother to take your 'at orf. It's orl right Master 'ardy," says the crafty grocer, by which time the poor old man couldn't get out fast enough.

Now the grocer never accused the man of the theft, but he told his neighbours and customers all about it with great glee. And they, even the children, started to call after him, "Mornin' Master 'ardy. Cold mornin'," till it got on the old man's nerves and he threatened to "make a hole in the water". Then everyone felt it had gone far enough and people stopped calling after him. But he always avoided the Top Shop after that.

The proprietor of this shop used to buy one gallon casks of whisky. When the cask was empty he would put in two or three pints of water and let it stand for about three weeks. The cask was so impregnated with the whisky that the resulting liquid, which was called roudle, made a very stimulating drink. This he would give to his friends.

One cold morning an old woman came to get her groceries and the shopkeeper asked her if she had ever tasted roudle.

"Never heerd tell on't,", she said.

So he gave her a glass and she pronounced it "Werry nice."

"Would you like another taste?"

"Well, thank 'ee but puttin' on good natur' I wouldn't mind."

No sooner had the second glass been downed than the old lady collapsed and had to be carried home. Roudle is indeed a powerful concoction.

There was a little cottage shop popular with us schoolchildren at the bottom of the Green in the tall, narrow three-storied house. It looks like one house, but has two front doors and a long path in front. In the front room of the one nearest the school an invalid man, Bob Barker, sold sweets and a few toys.

For the few weeks coming up to Christmas just before my fifth birthday we used to stop and gaze longingly in the window. There I saw a little Noah's Ark. I'd learnt all about the animals going in two by two and thought how much I should like to have that ark. One day I dared to ask the price. It was sixpence. Christmas came and I could hardly believe my good luck when an aunt gave me a whole sixpence. No sooner did Boxing morning arrive than I dashed off down the road and bought that Noah's Ark. How thrilled I was and how carefully I handled it as I slowly walked back up the casey with my new toy. I couldn't wait to get home to open it, but sat on my favourite seat at the top of the Green and began poking open the lid. Out came a collection of wood shavings, more and more, and finally a flimsy cardboard dog and a queer-shaped elephant. And that was all. I couldn't hold back the tears in the intensity of my disappointment. I was completely stunned. Finally I went home, but all Ma said was, "Well you shouldn't have spent all your money at one go."

There was an old bootmaker in the village with the same name as myself, though he was no relation to us. He lived with his wife and daughters in a small cottage at Holland at the back of the bakery. The cottage was on a slope and in very wet weather water poured in at the front door, ran through the cottage and out at the back. He was an old army bootmaker, a veteran of the Crimean War. He had a big mop of thick white hair, side-whiskers and a very long beard nearly down to his waist. He had several medals and I listened with fascination to the tales he told of how he won them, as I sat on a little stool in his kitchen while he worked.

I never did find out with any accuracy which countries he had visited. I sometimes doubted whether he knew himself.

They were all "furrin parts". The warlike "Rooshuns" and bloodthirsty "Urbs" (Arabs) figured largely in his tales, which grew more and more blood-curdling as I sat there open-mouthed, taking them all in. I never knew whether to believe him or not. Normally speaking he was not a liar (no more than most men), and he repeated tales with such conviction they rang true. While he was telling these exciting stories he used to put bunches of nails in his mouth and extract them one by one through all those whiskers. I marvelled at this feat, and even more at the fact that he never, as far as I know, nailed or sewed his beard to the boots he was making.

There were a lot of independent, self-employed people in the village. In a cottage near my bootmaker friend, Miss Heard ran a little school for small children. Later she moved to a bigger house in Church Row. There were two other small schools in Melford at this time. One was run by Mr. Payne, a learned gentleman who lived in Hall Street at what later became the manager's house of Lists Horsehair Factory. One of his pupils was the well-known socialist Mr. Sidney Webb, who became Lord Passmore. The other school, at the corner house opposite the side entrance of the Bull, was run by Mr. Hurst, father of Bernard, and formerly headmaster of Cavendish Grammar School. He was a clever Greek scholar.

As already mentioned, we had a farrier and blacksmith, Mr. Sparrow in Westgate Lane, as well as a whitesmith, Mr. Downs. There were two other blacksmiths in the village, Mr. Codling at Little St. Mary's, and Mr. Brockwell next to what is now Young's Garage.

I was specially fond of visiting Mr. Brockwell's shop, with the fine lime trees in front. He was a very kind man and never minded us boys hanging round his trav'us watching the sparks

Little St. Marys, Codling's forge, c. 1895.
From print owned by Cyril Youngs, Esq.

fly and seeing all the animals shod – great big shire horses right down to the little ponies. Mr. Brockwell became warden at the Hospital when he retired, and when his workshop was pulled down two houses were built on the site.

We had saddlers and harness-makers in the village and, like the blacksmiths, they always had plenty of work. Mr. Deeks and Mr. Neave were both saddlers. We had a brush-maker too, Mr. Richold, who had a place in Hall Street, near the Bull. There was a rope-maker who had a shed at the back of the Bull, named Salter. He was a little old man and he had a boy to help him in his business. He tied thick bunches of flax loosely round his waist and used to spin it out in front of him. It always reminded me of a spider. He used to walk backwards from a machine which twisted the material and formed ropes. I often watched him working and was fascinated by it, but couldn't fathom how he did it.

There was always a great deal of activity around the Bull. It was of course the stopping place for coaches and carriers' carts of all types, and riders on horseback too would draw up there for rest and refreshment. They'd shout to the ostlers to attend their mounts, and small boys would hang around hoping to pick up a copper or two by holding a horse's head. At the stables at the back there was always a great deal of activity and interest. The pump was in constant use. Sometimes a weary traveller or a gentleman who had over-indulged in drink would give a boy a halfpenny to work the pump while he held his throbbing head underneath the cold water. And it really was lovely water, both to wash in and to drink.

We had a foundry too, run by Messrs. Ward and Silver

Bull Hotel from Mat Factory window, c. 1900. Meeting of hounds. The man in cart at the left corner is Dennis Reeve. *Photo by E. Ambrose*

(where the Co-op now stands) where wheelwrights and wagon-makers produced some of the finest work in the country. Timber was laid out there for years to make quite sure it was properly seasoned. Men working there took a tremendous pride in their products. They were splendid craftsmen, almost artists, producing every kind of equipment for an agricultural community. One of their wagons, when forty years old, was sold for £60, a considerable sum of money in those days.

Further up the road (next to what is now Oliver's shop) were the coachbuilders, two brothers named Richold. One of them, Sam (who was in the choir with me for several years) told me they would put twenty-one coats of paint on a coach. They had a very high standard of craftsmanship. The Richolds were a fine old family and well-respected in Melford. One of them went out to South Africa and founded a big business like Maples, and I have seen a fine picture of it with a tall flagstaff on top.

There were two horsehair factories in the village, one was Lists in Hall Street and the other one was at what is now called Vieille Maison, formerly the Old Tea House. Quite a few of the villagers had looms in their own homes where they did work to supply these factories. I remember Jack Stock having a great horsehair loom in his cottage which took up half the living room, and I've known of very little children having to sit alongside these looms picking out one black and two white hairs (or whatever was required) and handing them to their mothers (very often the women did this work) for hours on end. They worked what hours they liked, often very late, no doubt to the detriment of their eyesight. Women and children mostly did this work while the men were out on the farms.

Many people worked very long hours. I can remember a stonemason who lived up High Street. He used to walk four miles to work every day at Keoghs in Sudbury, and four miles home at night. He was a very good mason, but one rarely saw him out except on his way to and from work.

Nearly everyone had a go at helping themselves and trying to earn a bit extra, to make ends meet. The wife of a mat-maker I knew used to make very good toffee and sell it to earn a few extra pence. Many of the women took in washing or did needlework of some sort or another. There was always plenty of sick nursing (though this was rarely paid for in cash, more often in kind, such as a few potatoes). Grandma acted as midwife (very much in demand in those days), and when I got older I was glad enough to earn two shillings and sixpence playing for a smoking concert or a convivial evening. One of the mat-makers named Adams kept bees and made a bit extra selling his honey. You could buy a comb for sixpence – a great treat. I loved watching him take the honey out of the container and always asked when he was going to do it so that I could come and see. He'd fling the container round and round and out came the honey, right hot and sticky. He'd give me a chunk to take home.

I remember Charlie Olgar, the postman, who earned a bit extra by acting as our town crier. He went round the village ringing his bell and calling out all sorts of announcements such as things lost or found, strayed animals, meetings of all sorts. He charged a penny a time for this service, and also a penny a time for being knocker-up. For this he used a long pole with a knob of bristles on the end to rattle on bedroom windows. He'd call out: "Wake up, wake up, nice fine morning." He was a rare skater and we used to watch him on Clappits pond skating backwards and doing figures of eight. This impressed us boys tremendously.

We had two maltings in the village which also provided work, and there was the mat factory, but I will write in more detail about that later. A lot of men in the village worked with horses, as was only to be expected in a community where we all relied on horse power. These men loved their charges. They knew and understood them and because they lived in such close contact with them, many were quite capable of acting as vets, should the need arise. The coachmen, especially those employed by the big houses, were very proud of their horses, and saw to it that both they and their equipment were turned out in perfect order, with shining harness and trappings.

I remember Walter Mayes, a coachman and groom, who was an expert with horses. Frank Boreham was another skilled man. He was a trainer and we'd often watch him at work on the Green, patiently breaking in a young horse on a long rope. Dennis Reeve, too, was another specialist, but he worked on farms and was a very experienced cattle man. They were a fine crowd and I admired their skill.

In a country district such as ours there were of course a great many farm labourers. These men were classed as unskilled labourers, but I always felt they were worthy of a far better status. They were very proud of their work and boasted about their skill in ploughing a straight furrow. They had ploughing matches and were dead keen on winning. On Sundays they would walk round inspecting each other's work in the fields, and especially on allotments which many of the men had, and would criticise without mercy when they met in the pubs.

We also had a few mole-catchers and I always looked on them as skilled men though they never seemed to have a very high rank in society. They were clever at their work with their home-made traps. From the moleskins their wives would make lovely caps and "weskits", warm, hard-wearing and waterproof.

The whole village was a closely knit community and we all knew each other's business. If a tragedy befell a family there was always someone on hand to come to their assistance; uncles, aunts, cousins and grandparents were all within reach. If no relation was able to help a friend would invariably step in, especially if a child was orphaned. My grandparents befriended such a child and brought him up as one of their own. It was a commonplace thing to do in those days. If someone grew too old or ill to work, very often friends or relatives would rally round and help to avoid them being sent to the workhouse. Everyone had a dread of the spike – the last step before the grave. They could of course apply to the Board of Guardians for parish relief (the Gardeens as they were usually called) but they got precious little help from them.

The livelihood of quite a lot of the villagers was closely connected in some degree or other with the manor houses of Melford and Kentwell. I suppose when I was very young we in Melford were still living in the last remaining stages of the old feudal system. All our needs were available in our own little community and we were completely self-reliant and self-supporting. Workmen requiring tools for their trade relied considerably on their own inventiveness or else on the skill of the local blacksmiths.

5

More about my Childhood

As a small child my chief area of activity lay between the Church at the top of the Green and the school at the bottom. There were always plenty of interesting things going on up my end of the village, but down the street there were many more people about.

In Hall Street there were quite a lot of small thatched cottages nestling close together, and old houses with overhanging upper storeys. At these cottage doors, especially on summer evenings, groups of women would stand, with arms folded, chatting with their neighbours, while from inside one could so often hear the dismal cries of small children and babies. Some of the older women still wore their hair in ringlets (which for some reason always fascinated me), and some talked with hard loud voices, shouting across the wide road.

Around nine o'clock the little groups melted away and out came quite a procession of women, and children too, with little jugs in hand going off to their favourite pubs for their supper beer, a penny for half a pint. I used to fetch Grandma's from the Black Lion. The publican was a very kind man and I discovered that if I said please and thank you and raised my cap to him, he would give me a little cake out of a stone jar he kept on his shelf.

There were a lot more trees and bushes around the Green at that time, especially round the old pound. The pound itself had been moved by this time and straying animals were impounded in a shed in Bull Lane opposite the back entrance to the pub.

The whole village was much more alive with birds and small animals of all kinds. Rabbits, hares, weasels, stoats, moles, hedgehogs, foxes, and snakes, and many more were there in abundance. I am afraid we schoolchildren treated them all with indifference and thought they were there for us to destroy. The farmers too were no better and as soon as any strange creature appeared on their land they were ready with their guns.

The village green was our playground and we shared it with the sheep, donkeys, horses and cattle which happened to be using it at the same time. Early one Sunday morning I was playing at the top of the Green when a young horse suddenly kicked up his hind legs and gave me a severe cut on the forehead. Bleeding profusely I ran home. In alarm my father ran the whole way down the street to the doctor, jumping straight over the railings in his haste. Fortunately the doctor was at home and was quickly on the job, putting some stitches in my head. I still have the marks of that horse's hoof.

We were very fortunate in living in a district where there were so many fields and woodlands, brooks and streams where we could play. We had no organised games at school at all, so we made up our own. We had spinning tops of sorts, mostly home-made with an old cotton reel and a thick nail, and we'd spin our tops from home right down the casey to the school yard. A few of us had hoops, and a few marbles, and the girls had skipping ropes, but we mostly made up our own games and our own rules. Jump Billy Wagtail was popular among the boys. Two boys leaned against a wall, the next boy had to jump on to their backs, then followed all the rest till the whole row collapsed. We were always kicking a ball about on the Green. The ball was usually a home-made affair, but it served our purpose. I can remember playing at football till darkness fell and the moon appeared.

One source of great joy to us was to play around the mill stream by the old ford, which was still in use for horse traffic. There were large stepping stones there and we would have great fun trying to move them. In this shallow stream there were lots of dabchicks and voles, newts, frogs and of course lots of small fish much enjoyed by the kingfisher and the heron, or harnser as we called him.

I loved to stand and watch the kingfisher with his fine head and long beak, his brilliant blue colouring flashing as he suddenly darted into the water and invariably returned to his perch with a fish in his beak. At nesting time they were wonderful as they prepared the nest in the bank, working together. And I loved to see the courting, when the cock bird would bring presents of little fish and give them to the hen. Then later on, their busiest time of all, when they brought little fish to feed their young. I never cease to admire these charming birds.

We boys prided ourselves on throwing stones at all these little creatures and were very proud if we succeeded in being accurate enough to kill a bird on the wing. Though I was never specially good at this I joined in the fun and one day I threw a stone and killed a kingfisher in flight. When I went to pick it up I was so disgusted with myself for taking the life of so beautiful a creature I vowed to myself I would never kill another living thing. I think this little incident made me all the more interested in kingfishers.

There was one bird though we boys would never kill and

that was the robin. We said it would bring bad luck. And we would never kill a ladybird. We called this a rainy bug, and said that if we killed it, it would assuredly rain! There were many superstitions about animals. The croaking of ravens always meant disaster; if the tawny owl hooted at night it meant certain death for someone; and if your cat was lively with "wind in his tail" that forecast rough weather.

Among many varieties of birds I remember as a child which were quite numerous were the greenshanks and redshanks, the corncrakes and several varieties of woodpecker. Kestrels and sparrowhawks were common and we often saw flocks of snipe flying over the meadows. There were many varieties of owls, guinea fowl and redstarts; there were yellowhammers down by the flax factory and butcher birds at Royden, nightingales in the fir trees in the school yard and little tree creepers, wrens and the fascinating oven birds. It was a shame we didn't appreciate them more than we did.

There always seemed to be plenty of things to do when we were children, depending of course on the season of the year. In winter we always got excited when the first snow appeared and I can still picture the thrill of little children (having myself reached the mature age of seven) on coming out of school and seeing the snow falling, and yelling with excitement, "Ere be a littl' 'ole 'ooman up there a-pluckin' the geese."

We'd always hope for a hard frost so that we could go sliding on the frozen ponds or river. I remember we had a little schoolmate called Dummy Tatum, who had a wooden leg, but in spite of his handicap he was a great sport. We were playing one day at the mill dam when the water was frozen. We kept running across and back, daring each other to get there and back before the ice broke – very dangerous as the water was deep. Dummy wanted to join in too and he made to cross the dam, when splosh, his peg-leg broke the ice and in he went. We all rushed in after him and hauled him out, and I can still picture the sad little figure of Dummy stomping along with a lop-sided lurch, soaking wet, making for home. I hope he didn't get into trouble. He was a brave little fellow and we all liked him.

As the spring came along there were flowers in abundance, though we rarely bothered much about them as they were so plentiful and common. The girls did I suppose, but we left that to them. The countryside was alive again with bird and animal and insect life and we all seemed part of it. We would help snare in nets many of these little creatures for food. A favourite place was at the bottom of the old church tower, which was thick with ivy. We waited till nightfall, when sparrows collected there in abundance to roost, and we would gently drop a net down then pull it up sharply and soon had a lot of birds. We would spread nets on the fields and collect larks. Pies and puddings were made with these little birds. They were fiddly to prepare but made a lovely meal. All kinds of birds were used in this way – thrushes, fieldfares, blackbirds, as well as pigeons of course. Larks were very tasty. Plovers made a lovely pie too, and a golden plover was a special delicacy used to tempt the appetite of an invalid. The pie-crust was a thick mixture of flour and suet or dripping and water.

On Sunday mornings you'd see quite a procession of children going across the Green to the bakehouse with their Sunday pies. These were cooked in the still hot ovens for a penny a time. After church was over, about one o'clock, the procession would start again, this time with cloths in their hands to collect their pies. Sometimes the pies got mixed up and when you got home you found you had a rabbit pie perhaps instead of the pigeon one you'd sent. This mostly caused amusement, but if you were the loser it was not so funny.

We used to search for plovers' eggs, which were specially nice to eat. They were laid between the furrows and were not easy to find.

When summer came we had a high old time, playing cricket (of sorts) on the Green and running wild in the countryside, looking for birds' nests or animal haunts, climbing trees, collecting firewood and cones ready for winter again. We'd go swimming in the Hall Mill dam, or in the river or floodgates at Liston, and most of the boys taught themselves to swim in these waters. We'd go searching for crayfish in the pool near the old flax mill and bring them home for mother to cook for tea. This mill became Stafford Allen's Works and is now Bush, Boake, Allen Ltd.

We'd collect blackberries, sloes and mushrooms and fill our pockets with hazelnuts. We'd go searching in the pond in Kentwell Park for tiddlers, newts and frogs. Sometimes we'd come across an adder and often a grass snake, which the boys would instantly kill. We'd go down Hare Drift (where we often saw red squirrels) and play in the timber yard belonging to Melford Hall estate. Great tree trunks lay around as well as planks of all sizes. From these we'd make a tipney tauter as we called it, or titter me tauter – a see-saw. I can still recall the fun we got from this simple game and can hear in my mind the excited voices of the younger ones calling out, "This 'ere un bannals" (balances) as they successfully dragged a plank across a tree trunk to make a see-saw.

Another interesting thing to do was to follow the hunts, of which there were plenty in the season. Occasionally I would follow an otter hunt. The men dressed in blue suits and had very big rubber boots. They'd walk along the river up past Stafford Works on to Glemsford. They had special hounds for otter hunting. After a few trips following these hunts I gave up: it, was heavy going and I usually came home soaking wet, having seen nothing but mud.

Some of the boys would follow after the fox hunting, but I preferred just to watch the meet assemble. It was such a colourful spectacle, and I loved the hounds. One morning I went to see a meet at Kentwell Hall. We knew the butler there and he invited me in and gave me a rare good feast of boned and stuffed turkey. I can still recall how delicious it was and what a huge piece he gave me!

There were many grand shooting parties at the halls when I was a boy, and it was considered quite a normal thing to shoot 500 pheasants in one day. I'd go along with the boys to watch these shoots at Kentwell. We'd go down that long road on the far side of the Hall and from there we had a splendid view of the shooting. It was an exciting sport.

The highlight of the year was of course harvest time, which came during our summer holidays. We children took our part along with the adults and we all had a wonderful time together in the cornfields. Everyone in the village took a personal interest in it. It was such an important event, a culmination of all the work of the whole year, and both the church and the village celebrated the occasion with festivals and horkeys.

Most of the villagers would go gleaning, and many of them would gather enough corn to provide them with flour for many months. They would take the corn to the Hall Mill, or the mill on the Stansted Road, and there have it ground. This was a very big help where there were large families.

When Christmas time came round we used to gather evergreens to decorate our homes, not forgetting the mistletoe which we got in Kentwell Avenue. We'd watch with great interest the preparations for the feastings. On Christmas Eve we would hang up our stockings and wake early while it was still dark to get that thrill of feeling first of all what we had got. It was usually an orange, a few nuts, a tin whistle or spinning top, or a doll for the girls; and a few sweets, or suckers as we boys liked to call them – it sounded more manly!

These gifts were often all we got; we never had any big presents. Sometimes a relative would give us sixpence if we were lucky. A few gifts were exchanged by the adults in the family, a muffler or pair of braces, a belt or neck-tie. Some employers would give a present to their workmen, such as a piece of meat or poultry, or a bottle of wine. Families concentrated much more on feastings, and made much of their Christmas dinner. We had very few Christmas cards and because they were scarce we treasured them.

There would be family parties and these were quite big occasions lasting well into the night. There were bon-bons (crackers) with obscure mottoes which the adults laughed at, funny hats and bits of cheap jewellery. These parties seemed to be planned more for grown-ups than children. We just happened to be there, spectators to the antics of the adults but not encouraged to take much part in the show.

When I got tired of the jollity and the noise I would squat down in a corner, or else find a little ledge under the table and there I'd weave all sorts of imaginary tales to myself. I wouldn't feel in the least bit suppressed or frustrated. In fact I was very happy. Of course it was much more fun when my brother George was old enough to join me under the table, but he was

41

a master one for playing jokes and he'd prod the grown-ups' feet and legs which were just within our reach. He'd pretend to be a mouse and scare the ladies. Then we'd get into trouble and probably be sent off to bed, where we'd soon fall asleep to the sound of the merry-makers staggering out of the Black Lion singing lustily and shouting to one another, and to other groups rolling across the Green from the Hare, while from down below strains of jolly ditties mixed with Christmas carols came wafting up the stairs from our own family party.

There was a lot of poverty in the village when I was a boy and many of the children who were at school with me came from wretched homes. There were a lot of large families with seven or eight children, in spite of the fact that many children died in infancy. Often parents couldn't afford the penny a week for their schooling and the children stayed away for that reason, or because they hadn't any boots to wear. I remember some of them being sent into the fields as "scarecrows", to walk up and down the fields rattling a tin with stones in it all day, for the magnificent sum of sixpence a week.

Many of them had long walks to school from outlying parts of the village. They would sometimes arrive in wet clothes and if they got there early enough would hang round the open fires trying to get dry. They would bring a little hunk of bread and dripping for their dinner, but would more often than not eat it on their way to school. In the dinner time they would wander into the fields at the back of the school looking for something to eat, perhaps a turnip or swede. We all used to eat all sorts of things we found in the fields – berries and leaves and plants. It's a wonder we were not poisoned. Perhaps some of us were. I often heard of someone having colic, a general term used for stomach upset.

42

I always felt sorry for the children who had "to stay to dinner", especially those who came from poor homes. I was lucky and could run home to Mother, who always had something good to eat and who would dry my clothes if they were wet. I learnt at a very early age that a child's health and happiness depended so much on a mother's care and good management, most especially if they were poor.

There was so much drunkenness when we were small, the pubs being open from six in the morning to midnight. Beer was cheap at twopence a pint and some men would drink beer for breakfast and not bother about food. It was a bad thing when the man of the house was always tipsy, but far worse when the woman was. I saw so many tragedies because of this.

Partly because of this heavy drinking and partly because of the poverty, consumption was rife. Many of the working people had insufficient food and easily succumbed to the disease. Hygiene too was very poor; indeed the word hadn't been heard of, and would have been laughed at if it was suggested. Smallpox too was not unknown and everyone dreaded it. As soon as anyone contracted it they were rushed off to isolated houses in the woods.

Because of their poverty most country folk only consulted the doctor as a last resort, after having tried their own remedies first, with the help of friends and neighbours. Some of these remedies were very simple and extraordinarily effective. If we children had a sore place or an open wound, Ma would let a dog lick it; the saliva of a young healthy dog was considered very good for healing sores and wounds. Cobwebs were put over cuts to stop bleeding and this was mostly effective. Women would cut a large onion in half and put it under the bed to "counteract diseases". They claimed the disease would

43

fly to the onion!

Herbs of course were in constant use; camomile tea for colds and chills; boiled nettles to clear the blood. For asthma the women would gather coltsfoot, thyme and horehound, boil it gently, adding glycerine to the liquid. It tasted good and soothing. Elderflower boiled and sweetened with treacle was given for feverish colds, and the white fluid from dandelions squeezed on warts to get rid of them. There were many other obscure treatments for warts. A cure for boils was to boil a few pellets from poachers' cartridges (small shot lead type), make up a poultice and apply to the boil. As there was lead and manganese in these small shots I suppose they might have had some beneficial results.

Thrush was a common condition among babies and even older children. For this a mother would get a few nails from the blacksmith and put them in water. When the nails were thoroughly rusty she would wipe the child's mouth with a rag dipped in the water. A remedy for rheumatism was to carry a pair of mole's feet (must be front feet though) as close as possible to the affected part. Another cure for thrush was crushed snails, tied up in a piece of rag and given to the child to suck.

Snails were rather a popular remedy and used a lot, crushed and used as a poultice or allowed to crawl over the injury. I've heard of children being given fried mouse for whooping cough, but Mother never inflicted that on us, so I don't know what it tasted like. But she did give us – pretty regularly too – brimstone and treacle. She'd put it on a spoon and "Open your mouth," she'd say, and down it had to go, like it or not. Leeches were still in use and these could be obtained from the chemist, who kept them in big earthenware jars with holes in them.

6

More about Schooldays

When I was seven years old (in 1885) there was a great deal of unrest in the village. Groups of workmen would gather round the pubs in angry mood, and fights became more than usually vicious. Though I didn't understand very much about it, I heard talk about the mat-makers in Melford, as well as those in Glemsford and Lavenham, being on strike for more wages. This was a desperate action to take in those days, as no money at all would be going into the homes and this meant starvation. At the same time a general election was imminent and this made feelings run higher still.

Glemsford at that time was a stronghold of liberalism while Melford was very largely Tory, and the antagonism between the villages was strong and often bitter. The men of Melford jeered at the Glemsford men, calling them Egyptians, and said they were outsiders. The words Egypt and Glemsford were so synonymous that the confusion spilled over into our geography lessons; and when a Sunday school teacher asked where the baby Jesus was taken when Herod threatened to kill all the babies, the answer came promptly: Glemsford!

Under a recent Parliamentary Reform Act the Glemsford men were demanding a polling station in their own village, instead of having to come to Melford to vote. When Polling Day (Tuesday 1 December) arrived and this was still refused, a body of mat-makers from the Kolle Matting Factory, led by their foreman on horseback, Henry Cook, came marching into Melford to demand their rights. They came along Westgate Street and broke some windows at the Scutchers Arms, then marched on down the road past the conduit into the village. They were armed with sticks and staves and were in a very militant mood. They recorded their votes then threatened to break up the polling station, which was at the Lecture Hall (now the Working Men's Club). Some of them swore they'd have my father's blood because they thought he was on the side of the owner of his factory. Father was foreman at the Melford Mat Factory and had tried to persuade the men there not to go on strike.

The Melford men were of course all out on the street, and when they heard the Glemsford men were marching into the village they joined together in a body preparing to fight the opposition. The situation began to look very ugly, with stones flying about and many windows broken. At this point Captain Bence of Kentwell Hall, a magistrate, read the Riot Act outside the Lecture Hall where the worst of the trouble-makers had collected. But the situation still remained very tense and dangerous.

The Melford police then appealed to the Sudbury police for help, but apparently they were unable to do so; probably they too had trouble on their hands with election activities. So they sent an urgent message to Bury, and the whisper went round the village "The red coats are coming!" Before very long a contingent of militia were sent by train. They were paraded on the station square, then ordered to fix bayonets. They marched up the long street, clearing out all the public houses on their way. At the sight of the militia in their red uniform stolidly marching up the street things quietened down very quickly.

When Pa came home later on we heard that the Glemsford mob had tried to manhandle him and would have beaten him up, but he escaped by dashing into the Crown Inn and, with a group of others including the landlady, Mrs. Clayden, scrambled out at the back and came home cautiously across the back fields. When he got to the Black Lion he recognised one of his most malicious attackers and was just going in after him when a policeman stopped him.

"I just want to give that bugger a sole of the skull. You know me," says Pa. "I shan't make a fuss. Just want to get my own back."

"Be quick about it then," says the policeman, "and give him one for me."

And Pa did too. His fist could land a pretty heavy one when he liked to exert himself.

The village street was in a sorry state after it was all over, with broken glass everywhere. Shops and public houses down the whole length of the street from Whittle's Mat Factory right down to Branwhite's brewery on Chapel Green had their windows smashed. The Crown Inn suffered most damage as the mob stormed inside and wrecked the premises. Compensation for this alone amounted to £137 15s 6d, a considerable sum at that time.

As I grew older I was joined at school by my brother George and later on by Jack. Among our friends were families of children who lived near us in Church Row, especially Fred and Harry Steed, as well as all the children who came from High Street. We were a noisy crowd when we were let loose from school, probably due to the fact that school life was largely one of suppression and stern discipline.

I can still recall the suppressed excitement on Friday afternoons. Three of us, Tipney Theobald, Harry Steed and myself, great pals and leaders of many schoolboy adventures, would plan to make a quick dash immediately the closing bell rang. We'd rush to the front door before any of the others could get there and slam the door behind us. As it opened inwards the oncoming crowd of boys would get blocked solidly behind the door, and get stuck. Pandemonium broke out. We'd stay around long enough to hear the uproar and to hear teacher descending upon the scene, threatening dire consequences on the perpetrators of the little game. By the time the door was opened and the class allowed to disgorge we were well out of sight. We made sure, however, to reserve this little game for Friday nights only, as we calculated that by Monday morning teacher would have forgotten the incident and we would be safe.

I can recall a great deal of fighting among the boys. For myself I was not particularly robust and mostly hung back, but occasionally I got caught up in some quarrel and would square up to a boy. We'd glare into each other's eyes and threaten calamity. We were probably both scared stiff. I know I was. After screaming threats of annihilation we'd take a pace or two back, ready for attack. Usually my brother George would appear at this point and we'd both retire. George revelled in fighting and would do enough for both of us. He was always more than willing to defend me with his fists, even though he was younger than me.

When the boys wanted to pick a quarrel they'd give a quick punch on their opponent's nose and shout "'scar's blow"

(I imagine this meant a coward's blow). Then they'd clench their fists and roll them quickly round and round, grab the opponent's cap from his head, throw it on the ground and stamp on it. After this insult the fight would start in earnest, other boys taking sides and cheering on their favourite.

At other times, for no apparent reason at all, the boys from down the street (the south side of the bridge) would start fighting the boys from our side. Stones would fly in every direction and sometimes this would develop into quite a nasty affair. Then just as suddenly we'd all stop in our tracks, quietly drop any stones we had in our hands, and fade away with as innocent an expression as we could muster on our faces. We had caught sight of a big gentleman in navy blue uniform with a truncheon hanging at his belt. He was the terror of the village, who kept order simply by his very presence – our village policeman, Inspector Farthing.

The police at that time hadn't much paperwork to attend to. In consequence they were always walking about the village and knew everyone. Moreover they knew all the local horses and carts, so if ever a crime was committed, the criminal couldn't get far without being traced. Criminals in those days usually worked alone, not in gangs, and having almost no transport, were more easily apprehended.

As children we were brought up to fear and respect the law; and the law at that time was harsh and unforgiving. Both at school and at church we were taught very sternly and clearly what was right and what was wrong; there were no in-between paths. There was little sympathy, if any, for delinquents and not much allowance was made for adverse or difficult circumstances. This harsh teaching was enforced by the representatives of the law, the police, of whom we stood in great fear. They were mostly big, middle-aged men, chosen for their strength. They would give a child a cuff across the head if caught in wrongdoing, and if he went home and complained to his parents he would probably be told it served him right and might even get a second hiding from them, so he mostly kept quiet.

Very occasionally when a teacher at school or even a policeman was particularly savage, a parent, sometimes a mother, would appear and make a terrible fuss. If this happened at school we tried to hang around and listen to the outcome, but it was a rare occurrence.

There were two cells at our police station near Hall Mill, where law-breakers were kept, and every other Friday morning our local magistrates, Captain Bence and Mr. Almack, would attend to try the cases. There wasn't much crime in the village – mostly poaching – but if something more serious cropped up it caused quite a sensation. On these occasions a fierce-looking parson from Hartest, the Rev. Packer, would drive over in his pony and gig to assist in meting out justice. He looked very imposing in his top hat with gold watch and chain stretched across his ample proportions, with a fierce expression on his face as much as to say "I'll get you; all of you." He was the terror of the poachers, who hated to see him in court.

Our fear of punishment kept us on the straight and narrow way. It was common knowledge that even children could be condemned to prison for stealing quite a little thing such as a handkerchief or even a piece of bread. We heard of men being transported for stealing turnips. My father knew someone who was hanged for stealing a sheep, and a man who lived near us in Church Row was given seven years for setting fire to a haystack. We knew too that at the police station they had a cat o' nine tails and a birch and we knew quite well that these things were used occasionally. They also had handcuffs for bad men, and some small ones specially made for children. We knew too that man-traps were still used. We accepted all these things as facts of life, and we would scare each other with awful tales about them.

But in spite of all the dire threats and severe punishments hanging over evildoers we didn't always lead blameless lives. I remember going with a few friends down Hare Drift to buy milk at the farm. You could get three pints of skimmed milk for a penny, a special cheap price if you went and fetched it, and Mrs. Coe, the farmer's wife, would give us children some to drink as well. We'd got the milk and were coming back through the farm when we saw some lovely ripe apples on the ground. We couldn't resist and promptly filled our pockets full. We felt very guilty, but very brave, until suddenly the farmer came along the narrow lane on horseback. We all politely raised our caps and squeezed ourselves into the hedge, hoping he wouldn't see our bulging pockets. He calmly went on his way, and we never knew whether he was just being kind to us or unobservant. We worried about that for quite a while.

When I was a boy, people in the village still talked about the murder of Maria Marten in the Red Barn as though it had only just happened, though it had actually taken place fifty years before I was born. The subject still cropped up in sermons as a terrible warning to evildoers. I should think it must have supplied parsons with subject matter for many years.

Grandma knew a man who had walked all the way to Bury with some of his friends to witness the hanging of William Corder. They started off the night before so as to get a good position. It was said 10,000 people attended to witness this gruesome sight, including women and children. It was on Monday 11 August 1828, which was a fine harvesting day, but gangs of reapers actually left their work to see the spectacle. Employers too had come, as well as large numbers of people of high rank, who arrived in carriages and gigs, so great was the attraction.

Another local sensation which made a deep and lasting impression was the public hanging of Catherine Foster. She was a young married woman who lived in a little cottage near the Church at Acton. She fell in love with another man and poisoned her husband by putting arsenic in his food. He vomited in the garden. A day or so later some of their chickens died and investigation showed that arsenic was the cause. They had eaten the vomit.

Mr. Robert Bixby, the baker in Hall Street, told me how he and a few friends had walked to Bury to witness this hanging. He said it was a deeply moving sight. The poor woman, who was only eighteen years of age, gave a heart-rending speech from the scaffold imploring other young women, who may be tempted as she was, not to follow her example, but to stand firm and stick to their marriage vows. Catherine Foster was the last woman to be hanged in public in Bury. This was in 1847. The last man to be hanged in this way was in 1851.

As I have said, the church and the school were closely connected and together they provided the background of our young lives. Though strict discipline was the order of the day, they also provided us with special treats. We always looked forward to Ash Wednesday, as we had a holiday on that day. But first we had to attend the service in Church. We would assemble at school at the usual time, then march in procession up the casey for the special service appointed for

Melford Church. Engraving by unknown artist, c. 1850.

Ash Wednesday, the first day of Lent, which as all churchgoers know is a Commination, or the denouncing of God's anger and judgements against sinners. This long and tedious service includes such exhortations as:

> Priest: Cursed is he that curseth his father or mother.
> Answer: Amen
> Priest: Cursed is he that removeth his neighbour's land-
> mark.
> Answer: Amen.

But having heard it before I knew that in the end it would all finish quite happily, and when we got to

> Priest: O Lord save thy servants
> Answer: That put their trust in Thee.

Priest: Send them help from above.
Answer: And evermore mightily defend them.

I began to feel happier and knew that we were getting to the end. Of course we still had the sermon to sit through before we would be allowed to run home for dinner, and then spend a lovely long afternoon running wild in the fields and meadows surrounding our homes, picking flowers, bird-nesting, gathering wood or just kicking a ball about.

Another great occasion connected with the church which brought us much pleasure and excitement was the annual Sunday School treat held in the summer. For days beforehand we watched with increasing excitement all the preparations going on in Parson's meadow. As we lived near the church we could proudly report on the progress: the exact time when the large tents were erected by Taylors of Bury, and when the long benches and trestle-tables appeared, these being scaffolding borrowed from local builders.

When the great day arrived we assembled at school dressed in our best bibs and tuckers, all clean and smart to begin with. There were about 200 of us, and led by a drum-and-fife band from Glemsford, we all marched up the casey in our appropriate classes to the church. Here we had a service and all "confessed their manifold sins and wickedness" before listening to a sermon.

This was followed by sports in the meadow. These consisted of flat races, egg-and-spoon and potato races, and for the boys, obstacle races (through sacks and ladders) and the three-legged race. My brother George would practise for days beforehand, especially for the three-legged race, with his friends Bob Rising and Bob Wicks. He always counted on winning and worked out beforehand how he'd spend his prizes. The prizes were twopence, threepence or perhaps fourpence. Most of the children ran in the heavy boots which everyone wore, but George would take his boots off at the last minute and run in stockinged feet. This gave him an advantage, and more often than not he did win.

Stakes were marked out by pennants with class numbers from the rectory gate right down to the gate in Westgate Lane, and when the sound of the tea bell rang we all rushed to our appropriate number, where stood our teacher. Then we were marched into the great tents for tea. At this point bedlam was let loose and for once teacher didn't complain. But again the bell would ring and we had to subside for grace to be said, immediately to be followed by another uproar when one and all started banging their thick earthenware mugs on the bare trestle tables in anticipation of the feast to follow. This consisted of very weak tea, and piles of thick bread and a scrape of butter, then followed bread smeared with jam.

After this was consumed we were allowed to go for the cakes. These were thick slices of rather heavy puddeny cake with a sprinkling of currants. While tucking into the bread and jam the boys would look over the cakes and remark "I'm goin' ter 'av that 'un, there's more curnts in 't." But the currants were few and far between.

There was always a sentry posted on each table to see fair play. "I ain't a-goin' ta 'ave too much bread an' butter 'cos I want they cakes" was quickly squashed by the sentry who saw that everyone had their fair share. The children ate ravenously and noisily till at last such remarks as "Phew, I wholly fare full" were heard, but somehow there were always a few ready to eat up the crumbs. Gradually the noise began to subside, and finally, after grace was again said, we were let loose once more into the meadow.

Sports continued till late in the afternoon and extended to the Green in front of the Hospital where the smaller fry would be organised in playing such games as Ring-a-Ring-of-Roses; "Here's to a couple, I wish you joy, First a girl, then a boy", "Here we go round the mulberry bush", and so on. Finally energies began to wane, and tired and rather grubby little contestants were ready to wend their way back to their homes. But talk about the great victories won that day and the many near misses continued for many days afterwards.

7

THE CHURCH

When I was a boy there was always a distinctive feel about Sundays, quite different from any other day of the week. On weekdays the village was a bustling active sort of place, but on Sundays a deep peace descended upon it. Most people (except of course those who had cows to milk or animals to feed) got up later and dressed more leisurely, and those who possessed any put on their best clothes. Those who hadn't any best clothes gave their boots an extra polish, washed their faces a bit more carefully and smarmed down their hair with more care and a bit of extra grease. We boys were dressed up in stiff white starched collars – most uncomfortable, while the girls were crimped and curled and threatened with dire consequences if they spoiled their clean frocks and pinnies or great big hats.

In due course the church bells began calling the village to worship and we had time to watch the procession of people making their way up Church Row, and to note with special interest the arrival of carriages and pairs, of ponies and traps and gigs, and to find out who was attending church that day. There were big stables at the back of the rectory where the animals were rested and watered. Some farmers came on horseback and a few would leave their mounts at the Hare. My brothers and I were in the choir and we had to hurry off to the vestry to don black cassocks and white surplices. Father too was a chorister, so we had to behave ourselves.

The front rows of the pews just below the pulpit were reserved for the rector and his family and friends. The Rev. Martyn used to have a great many very distinguished guests and it was always interesting to see these fine people in the front. Immediately behind them were the people from the big halls and their entourage. Further back still sat the villagers. On the opposite side the front rows were reserved for the men from the Hospital. They used to march up to the church in single file, one behind the other, dressed in long black cloaks and top hats. The warden led the way looking very important, with an elegant black-striped shoulder cape over his cloak and a thick cord with big tassels to tie it with, to show his authority.

Brethren at Holy Trinity Hospital, c. 1880-5. Centre back row: Mr. Spilling (Warden). Right back row: Mr. Sharman (Deputy Warden). *From print owned by Mrs. Howe*

We were always amused at late arrivals, especially two sisters who were dressmakers. They made a habit of coming in late (to show off their fine dresses and grand hats, so the women said). They would wait outside till after the Confession (they'd not be allowed in till then) then march up the aisle, with a swish, swish, swish of their rustling, voluminous skirts. Often following behind them came a little old lady who was rather simple-minded. Like many another in the village, she used to have cast-off clothing given to her. On Sundays she would deck herself out in the most gaudy of them and put on the biggest bonnet with piles of decorations and as much jewellery as possible, including many bangles. One day, with a resounding clatter, her bracelets fell off her arm, and to the amusement of the congregation they were a bunch of curtain rings.

On Sunday afternoons we would all go for a walk together, a popular pastime for whole families. Kentwell Avenue was a great place for these promenades, with its three-quarter-mile-long avenue of lime trees, said to have been planted in 1678. At the top of the avenue on the left-hand side, the second or third tree from the top, were carved the initials and date of a man whose horse bolted and was killed at this spot. We'd point this out to each other and speak about it.

We'd always meet friends up the avenue and stop for a chat. We children of course would have liked to have run about and played, but this was Sunday and well we knew it! We had to keep quiet while the adults exchanged news and views, and whispered the latest scandal.

It was a great place for boy-meets-girl manoeuvring and this was watched with great interest. When a young couple started going out together for the first time they would stroll along, very solemnly, not even touching hands, but keeping a

Rev. C.J. Martyn and Ladies' Group in Rectory Garden, c. 1890.
Standing on left: Miss Mason; seated front left: Mrs. Manning;
seated centre front: Miss Constance Martyn (daughter);
standing right: Rev. Martyn.
From print owned by E. Ambrose

respectful distance from each other, sometimes hardly talking at
all in their first ecstatic thrill of "walking out". If the friendship
progressed they might on subsequent walks go as far as lightly
holding hands, and this was duly noted by their elders. If, in
due course, the romance ripened into a betrothal, the young
man would stick a pheasant's feather in his bowler hat (if he
possessed one; if not, in his cap) and then they would march
along proudly arm in arm. This was a sure and certain sign they
were engaged to be married, and in this way they proclaimed
their intentions to all and sundry. Then tongues began to wag.

Another favourite Sunday afternoon walk was down

Westgate Street and up the hill towards Stanstead. We passed the miller's house on the left and at the top of the hill opposite the road to Stanstead in a small paddock surrounded by a hedge we'd see a fine windmill. It was an ideal site on such high ground. We were friends of the miller and sometimes we would climb to the top of the mill, from where we could get a wonderful panoramic view of the country round, and could even see as far as Pentlow and Foxearth Churches.

Corn was ground at this mill for local farmers and housewives; it was always very busy when I was a boy, and did a very good trade. Unfortunately as the years went by trade decreased and the lovely windmill ceased to be needed. Finally it fell into disrepair and was taken down. I felt sad about it as I loved to watch the great arms going round, especially on a windy day, and listen to the roaring swish of the great powerful sails. We always enjoyed seeing the miller at work and watching him scrape and clean the great stones he used for grinding. But on Sundays we had to go on walking with our parents, on down towards Stanstead, then back over Kentwell Downs following the footpaths past Kentwell Hall and home for tea.

After tea it was church again. The evening service drew even bigger congregations than the morning, and we would again see the processions of people and the carriages coming up the casey to the great church. It was quite a sight on winter evenings to see the lights on the carriages bobbing up the hill, and from people carrying lanterns. People used to come from quite a distance, and on festival days such as Christmas, Easter and Whit, but most especially at harvest time, it was filled to capacity. Local parishioners had to get there early to get their favourite seats. There must have been 800 worshippers on these occasions, and sometimes I have even seen people sitting down the aisles and right into the doorway.

We were very fortunate indeed in having as our rector the Rev. C.J. Martyn. He and his family were very kind and very much loved and respected by all in the village, whether they were churchgoers, Methodists, or "devil dodgers" who went to both church and chapel, or indeed those who went to no place of worship at all. He was a jovial, good-hearted, fatherly man, a plump Pickwickian figure, with balding head and a great concern for the good of others. He never refused to give money, food or help to a beggar, and there were a large number of this fraternity at this period. Whenever he travelled by train he would always without fail give a generous tip to the train driver and guard and thank them for a safe journey. "Our lives are in the hands of these men you know," he would say. He practised in his daily life what he preached from the pulpit.

He was appointed chaplain to Queen Victoria and used to preach in London on special occasions. He was very friendly with my father and told him on one occasion that Mr. Gladstone was present. "Old Gladstone sat there," he said, "and I gave him some home truths." But he didn't tell father what the truths were. In his sermon on the Sunday preceding the arrival of the fair, he always gave us a few gentle reminders about behaving ourselves. "My dear people, I do trust all will go well and that no mishap will befall anyone." We all knew what that meant.

At one election time the crowd got out of hand (not an unusual occurrence) and the Rev. Martyn went in amongst them to try to pacify them. But some of the roughs clapped his hat over his face and the police made several arrests and carted them off to the station. The rector, in his habitual kindly manner, pleaded for them and said the poor fellows just got excited and that he refused to prosecute.

The Rev. Martyn built St. Catherine's Church in memory of his wife, naming it after her, because he said it was too far for people to walk all the way up to the big church at the far end of the village. At the same time he had the small school built on for little children, as he felt the village school was too far away from the lower end of Melford for mothers to carry their little ones, or for them to walk. His thought and care for his parishioners was amazing, and whenever he saw a need he would find some practical way of meeting it.

The Rev. Martyn was keenly interested in the choir and did all he could to encourage all the members, even the youngest recruit. Every year he organised a choir outing to London, which he paid for entirely out of his own pocket. He would hire a complete train (which could be done for £25 at that time) to take the choir and a large number of parish workers as well, to some special exhibition or place of interest.

The train journey itself was a great treat, as for many people this was the only time they travelled by train. On arriving at Liverpool Street Station we'd all troop out of the station and climb into horse-drawn buses. These were open-topped, so if it was raining you were unlucky. But many of us liked to go on top, as from there you could admire the busy streets and the great buildings and shops, and enjoy the amusing backchat of the hansom cab drivers perched high up in their seats, flourishing their whips and shouting witticisms to each other.

After we had arrived at our destination we'd have a look round, then partake of a handsome dinner. Later on in the day we were given a high tea, to which we all did justice – and all of this at Mr. Martyn's expense. It was always a most exciting day's outing. Invariably, however, when we reached Liverpool

Street for the return journey home, two or three of the more adventurous gentlemen of the party would be missing, having "got lost" in order to have a night in town. The rector was always terribly concerned about this and would send telegrams trying to find out their whereabouts, but in vain. They would turn up next day, having thoroughly enjoyed themselves.

I was invited to join the choir when I was seven years old. Mr. Phillips, our school headmaster, who of course knew us all well, was the church choirmaster. Mr. Bernard Hurst, a very fine accompanist, was the organist. He later became choirmaster on Mr. Phillips' retirement. From these two gifted men we received excellent tuition and were able to produce a high standard of music.

We did choruses from oratorios and would tackle quite difficult and complicated music. There were twenty boys and twelve men in the choir at that time, and they could certainly hold their own in competition with local choirs. There were several fine choirs in the neighbourhood at that period, especially at Sudbury and Lavenham. We used to think the Sudbury choir boys were wonderful. They wore mortar boards with tassels – most impressive – and we wished we could! It was a matter of pride and some prestige to be a member of the church choir, and we had several families of fathers and sons. In due course my two brothers joined, so, with father, our family could boast of four choir members. But we were not alone, as Mr. Harry Bell also had three sons, George, Bert and Bob.

I always enjoyed choir practice. We were taught carefully and thoroughly. I soon learnt to read music and quickly grew to love it. I had an alto voice and was fortunate in having tuition and help in developing it. Music became the great passion of my life and memories of my early introduction to the beauty and majesty of great music are some of my most happy ones. Sermons at that time were very long and tedious and rarely seemed to have any relevance to our young lives, so it was not unusual for some of us to occupy the time by screwing up little balls of paper and throwing them across the chancel to the boys opposite, and being poked in the back by our seniors sitting behind us, or having our ears clipped for whispering. Having got tired of playing such little games, which were very difficult under such restrictive conditions, we'd give up trying and fall asleep.

I remember one specially hot evening when a small boy went sound asleep. He must have had a bad dream for he woke up with a sudden start and shrieked out loud, flung out both his arms, hitting the boys on each side of him a resounding blow on the face. You can imagine the commotion. All the boys burst out laughing. In the vestry afterwards we were admonished in no uncertain terms by the rector.

I can still recall sitting in those choir stalls as a very small boy. The beauty of the church and the richness of the music seemed to overwhelm me. It was all too wonderful to absorb. Other boys were just as impressed with the beauty of it all. We used to talk about it when we were in that frame of mind. The east window as well as those in the south aisle were filled with stained glass, and the clerestory too had coloured glass. On bright sunny days the sun shone through all this glass like some kaleidoscope or magic lantern and produced a brilliant effect. At certain times of the year one particular figure shone out more magnificently than the rest and seemed as though it was coming down towards me to lift me up into all that brilliance.

When I wasn't revelling in the beauty of the coloured

windows, or playing about with the other boys, my thoughts were wandering back into the past. We were taught in school about our local history, so the names of our church's benefactors were familiar to us. And sitting there so close to the massive, elaborate memorials made me wonder what sort of men and women they were, who lived so many hundreds of years ago. I wove all sorts of fancy theories about them, and loved to picture what life was like in Melford when they had wild boar in the parks and great hunting parties at the big halls. I'd have liked to have been around when Dowsing came to Melford to smash up the "idolatrous images" in the church, old Crumly Bumly's man we boys called him. I'd have helped to hide some of the precious and valuable church possessions.

I was always very fascinated by the story of the monk who used to live in that small narrow room between the chancel and the Lady Chapel behind the altar. When he lived there it was divided into an upper and lower floor, but the beams of the floor had fallen into ruins, so it was now one room and used as a clergy vestry. I wondered if he felt lonely in his cramped cell, saying prayers all day long for departed souls. I wouldn't have liked to have been a monk living there all alone.

There was a basement below this little cell with an old bricked-up fireplace and when workmen were making some alterations they discovered a flue above it and found in it the skeleton of a goose prepared for a meal. I often wondered why the monk hid it in the flue and whether he was called away in a hurry. Or perhaps he was going to enjoy a meat meal on some fast day and a superior called unexpectedly and he quickly hid his dinner. I wonder why he didn't come back for it. I liked to picture this old monk and wished I knew the answer.

I often used to think how exciting it would have been to

have lived in Melford on that great occasion in August 1578 when Sir William Cordell entertained Queen Elizabeth I at Melford Hall. I'd have loved to have been one of that retinue of 200 young gentlemen dressed in white velvet who, with 200 older ones in black velvet, to say nothing of 1,500 serving men on horseback, sallied forth to meet her majesty at the county boundary. I often thought about this when I played with my friends at the Hall bridge trying to re-arrange the big stepping stones there. No doubt there was only a ford at the time of Queen Elizabeth's visit, where the horsemen would cross, and pedestrians would probably have to use the stepping stones. I wondered if some of those dressed in that gorgeous white velvet got splashed and muddied as they crossed the stream. What sumptuous feastings they would have on this wonderful occasion. It would have been the talk of Melford for years to come!

Once a year we were rewarded for our labours in the church choir. On Christmas afternoon we all had to report to the church warden, Mr. Fisher (of Fisher and Steed the solicitors). He lived at Falkland House on the Green. He was a fierce-looking military type of gentleman with a curled moustache, but he was very nice. We would be given an orange and some money. I don't know how the amounts were arrived at, but most of the boys got about fifteen or sixteen shillings. One year I got nineteen shillings, but I was the senior boy alto and aged nearly twelve. No sooner had we politely said "Thank you" and got outside than the arguments began. "'E got more'n me", "'E ain't worth that much". However we consoled ourselves with our oranges. Ma quickly took charge of the money; that was too much to carry round with you, though I was allowed to spend a little myself.

When I was nearly fourteen my voice broke and Mr. Hurst invited me to sit with him at the organ on Sundays. This was a thrilling experience for me, and my love, indeed my passion, for music rapidly increased. I watched his masterly performance on the great instrument and listened enraptured to the beauty and power of the music he produced, and studied carefully the way he brought out all those fine effects. I continued to think about it when I got home and worked out in my own mind how the combination of chords and effects were produced. I lived for music at that period and it was a wonderful experience.

I was extremely fortunate because at this time a lady who was interested in my singing offered to pay for me to have organ lessons. My hob-nailed boots were quite unsuitable for use on the pedals and I remember I had great difficulty in finding some more suitable footwear. In the end I managed to get some large and rather flappy slippers, which were at least one stage better than the boots!

I revelled in these organ lessons and lapped up all the knowledge I could get. I was of course very fortunate in living so near the church and being allowed to go there and practise whenever I wanted to. After I had had barely six months' lessons, Mr. Hurst was taken ill and he sent for me. He said he'd tried all round the district to get a substitute but had failed and that I must play the organ for the next Sunday's services. I protested vigorously that I couldn't do it. But he insisted and told me to get my father to stand beside me to pull out the stops when needed. So with fear and trembling I did. In the middle of it all I remembered the dream I had had when I was very small. It had come true in every detail.

8

MELFORD FAIR

The highlight of the year in Melford was our annual Whitsuntide horse fair. As soon as winter was over we all began to look forward to it with mounting excitement. We schoolchildren had a special holiday on the Thursday and Friday, and even farm labourers were allowed some time off during the fair, a great concession in those days of hard work and few holidays.

Everyone went to the fair. It was the meeting place for all classes. The grand folk and the gentry in their top hats and smart frock coats; the bowler-hatted tradesmen and farmers and up-and-coming citizens of some repute; and the cloth cap wearers, the masses of unskilled (and often illiterate) workers. We all knew the class to which we belonged – clearly indicated by our headgear. But for the few days of the fair we all rubbed shoulders together and for the time being forgot our status in society.

As we lived at the top of the Green we were in an enviable position to see and hear all the goings-on. Excitement built up rapidly from the moment the first horse-drawn wagon arrived on the Wednesday afternoon to be in readiness for the opening on Thursday morning. We children raced up and down the street calling out to each other as we discovered fresh delights, such as some new roundabout or side-show.

Horses, ponies and donkeys poured in by the hundreds and swarmed all over the lower part of the Green. I knew a man named Bill Bantock from Preston near Lavenham who would bring as many as fifty to sixty horses for sale. Thursday was the day when most of the horse trading was done, and amongst the crowds were some pretty rough characters. Much in demand for work on the land were the Suffolk Punches, and there were always some very fine specimens of these lovely horses at the fair. The large groups of Welsh ponies too were very popular.

Buyers would stand looking at a group of animals, then point to one, perhaps in the centre of the pack. The dealer would dive right in amongst them, grab the wanted animal by the mane and pull it out with the greatest ease. Then he would run it up and down showing off its good points. Often a gentleman would bring his child with him and together they would choose a little pony or donkey for a pet. Carts and horses, buggies and traps and donkey carts were also on sale. It was a busy, bustling, noisy scene, with dealers shouting, buyers arguing, children laughing and shouting, and dogs all over the place joining in the melee. The animals would be trotted up and down the middle road, or alongside Bixby's bakery, and sometimes outside the Bull.

Buyers came from a very wide area, even from abroad. I met some from Germany and Holland. Knowledgeable buyers knew what points to look for and would study the animal carefully before making a deal, but occasionally a less experienced person would be taken in by slick sales talk and "sold a pup"; before he had time to complain, the dealer would have disappeared. One man bought a horse at the fair and when he got it home it refused to eat or drink. Resignedly he said, "Well you're the hoss for me if you do but work."

I remember one old horse dealer who was a regular visitor to the fair. He was a tough character and a hard bargainer, a man to be reckoned with. His name was Bill Pattle, a heavily built man, six foot four inches tall. He wore a very thick double-breasted coat with a picture of a horse on each breast pocket and one on the back. He wore a bowler hat and always carried a riding whip. He was very rough and almost always in a state of intoxication. He used to declare, "I was brought up under the wagon wheels." He had several sons who had hard work to keep up with their father. One day he was so dead-drunk in his cart they didn't know how to get him out. But his old woman wasn't bothered at all. "I'll show you. Take the hoss out of shafts; tip up the wagon an' jes' slide 'im out." From then on this was their usual method of getting father in and out of the wagon.

Melford Fair dealers, c. 1900. The big man in the tall hat is Bill Pattle, well-known dealer; the man in the bowler is Bodger Allen the butcher.
From print owned by E. Ambrose

There was always a very good exhibition of agricultural appliances put on by Messrs Ward and Silver, who were established where the Co-op now stands in Melford. Their displays attracted a lot of farmers and hundreds of pounds worth of business was done. A corner of a refreshment tent would be set aside for the dealers to complete their transactions. Whisky flowed freely and I can always remember a magnificent aroma of cigars round there.

There were always quite a few beer tents on the Green, run by various brewers. As they had large stocks of drink in them they would employ watchmen to keep guard during the night. One night my father and a few friends, having enjoyed a convivial evening at the Lion, decided to go and visit old Sippy Meggs, who was acting as caretaker at one of these tents. They crept in; all was silent. One of them struck a match, and there was old Meggs sound asleep under the table. They banged and rattled on the table, but there was no response. Sippy was too far gone. "Pity to disturb him," they said and left. Next morning they asked him how he got on the night before. "Phew. It wholly thundered and lightened last night." He'd no idea the lightning was caused by the match being struck, nor the thunder their thumping on the counter.

As well as all these beer tents on the Green, quite a few of the villagers who were in the habit of brewing their own ale used to hang a bough over their front doors during fair time to indicate they had beer for sale. These were called bough houses, and I've no doubt they did quite a good trade during fair time.

The amusement part of the fair was held at the top of the Green opposite our house, so we were right in the midst of it and got to know a lot of the regular fair people. My father was very friendly with old Mr. Barker and his wife, whose family had visited the fair for many years with their roundabouts and side shows, and whose descendants still carried on the old tradition under the name of Barker and Thurston. He was a fine old gentleman, very fond of classical music, and he would bring an improved type of organ to the fair every year. I loved to stand and listen to the music coming from his organs.

The earliest roundabouts I can remember were operated by horses who trotted round inside in a continuous circle. Small organs were then in use, a young boy patiently turning a handle. Later on, the steam engine took the place of horses, with much black smoke being emitted from the low chimneys. Then came the excitement of the "galloping horses" when the "horses" went up and down as well as round and round. Previously of course they just went round on the level.

Friday was always considered to be the fashionable day at the fair, when the people from Kentwell and Melford Halls, and other big houses in the neighbourhood, graced the occasion by their presence and brought their children to enjoy the fun. And the fair people saw to it that they were given courteous treatment and were well looked-after. No doubt they got a few nice tips in consequence. The more timid and "refined" of the village women would also come on this occasion, partly no doubt to see and mix with the gentry.

There were a wonderful variety of stalls and booths and side-shows for our delight and we children used to save up for weeks and compare notes as to how much we'd got to spend. "Ah've gotten threepence ha'penny" was a proud boast. For a penny you could get a little saucer of whelks or winkles or cockles soaked in vinegar, or a plate of peas, or a little slab of cold rice pudding. For twopence a large piece of fried fish and a hunk of bread, sold by Rolando, the Sudbury fish merchant, and half

Melford Melford Fair stall holders, c. 1900.
Photo by E. Ambrose

a pint of beer for a penny to wash it down. There was home-made candy and rock, made by slinging it over a big hook on the caravan, lots of brandy snaps, gingerbread men, cakes and buns, some even with a few currants in them. Some buns were a penny each with four divisions, and if you had only a farthing to spend they'd sell you one portion. Fruits and nuts of all sorts were on sale. "All sound nuts. I'll gie anyun' fourpence who ken find a bad 'un." My brother George, taking him at his word, said to the salesman, "I ken see two that 'ave got holes in." "Go away you nasty little boy!" was all he got for his pains. There were coconut shies at which my father excelled. Swings and flying trapeze (sliding down a kind of clothes line); "sea on land", "ships with sails", and Rolly Polly, which made me feel sick just to watch. There were swing-boats, switchbacks, hurdy-gurdies and merry-go-rounds.

There were lots of side-shows which always fascinated me. I

loved to stand and watch the touters standing on a stage in front of their booths, shouting out and trying to allure customers inside. There was the fattest lady in the world, whom we were allowed to touch or even pinch; the tiniest man or some other poor human with a grotesque deformity, much accentuated for the show. There were peep-shows, shooting galleries, fortune-tellers.

I had very little spending money but one day I was tempted into a booth by a man who kept shouting, "Walk up; walk up; come and see the moving pootigraphs, wonderful new discovery." I paid twopence and stumbled into a darkened tent, where I waited for some time before a few more patrons came in. Finally a photographic assistant arrived and, with many wordy explanations, started up a noisy contraption which ejected an occasional puff of smoke and there appeared some shadowy figures on the screen. It wavered and flickered, went off, then came on again. The second attempt was slightly more successful and figures moved several times, but after that effort it spluttered and went out. The proprietor came in and announced "Ladies and Gents. Please make no remarks, but just give a clap of the 'ands if you appreciate it." There were a few, very few, claps. I went out a bit sadly, wishing I'd never spent my twopence because at the next booth the man was calling out "Fish an' bread twopence. Come and fill yer 'ungry bellies."

We always had a few strolling players at the fair and every year without fail they would put on a new (or old) version of *The Murder in the Red Barn*, the heart-rending tragedy of Maria Marten. *Blandy's Ghost* was popular too. You always had to wait ages for these to begin because it took them a long time to get a full house. Performances lasted about half an hour and cost fourpence for the front seats and twopence at the back.

Another attraction was the Floating Lady. There was a kind of spectroscope manipulated by mirrors with lots of gilt frames arranged somehow so that the lady appeared to be floating, suspended in air. This was quite a big attraction. Then there was the menagerie, which consisted of a few wretched little animals such as rabbits, perhaps a monkey or two, a few marmots or similar little creatures. They appeared to be well looked-after. Having persuaded a few spectators to come inside, the proprietor became the narrator and walked round with them, giving expansive dialogue on "these most uncommon animals and their 'abits." "This 'ere wild cretur burrers in the 'ut" (earth) and so on. Very illuminating!

There were always a few tricksters at the fair, performing the three-card trick or the three half crowns in the purse. I've seen this done so often, but could never fathom how it worked. They would hold up three half crowns and would slowly drop them into the purse, then offer it for sale at half a crown. By the time you bought one and looked inside there were three pennies in it. But the police were always around and these gentlemen didn't stop long.

Pickpockets abounded, but as most of us had so little to lose we didn't worry much. These men came with the sole object of stealing. They worked in little groups. They were very polite, would ask the time or for a match, while their accomplice deftly relieved the victim of his watch or wallet. They looked on it as a sport and were very successful.

My brother's favourite place was the boxing booth. This was a fairly large tent with a stage in front. On this stood two or three prize-fighters, ferocious-looking gentlemen, with huge muscular bodies, stripped to the waist, wearing extra large boxing gloves, standing there with arms folded and a threatening scowl on their big faces. The proprietor would use a large circular contraption like a trombone which, when worked up and down, would send a loud fog-horn like hooting noise all over the ground. By this means he'd attract a crowd then announce in a bellowing voice, "Ladies and Gentilming, come in an' see the finest fighters in the world. Come in an' see a genu-ine blood fight. I'll gie 'alf a croon to anyone who kin stand up to one on 'em for three rounds." If anyone offered he would fling out a pair of gloves and the half crown and get the contestant into the tent. An admiring crowd would follow, paying fourpence at the tent door, hoping to see plenty of blood flowing! Then came the announcement "In the red corner Mr. ...... and in the blue corner, the pride of Melford, your very own Mr. ......"

Occasionally a dark horse would appear among our locals and if he looked likely to out-box the professionals, the proprietor would shorten the fight and give the challenger a shilling. He didn't want his men to get knocked about. Amongst our Melford men we had some quite celebrated fighters (and fighters is the right word to use, not boxers). There was Pudney Sillitoe, Dally Olger and Jack Jocelyn, all more than capable of holding their own with the professionals. Sippy Meggs too was a good boxer and was often invited by a rector of a neighbouring village to a training bout of boxing for which he would pay him two shillings and sixpence.

My father had a great sense of humour and one day he was standing at the back of the crowd when the boxing booth proprietor was inviting challengers. To everyone's surprise, Father suddenly said he'd have a go. The gloves and half crown were thrown out to him and he made his way inside the tent.

When the onlookers realised what was happening they flocked in. "Come on. Let's see what old John 'ull do." The crowd rushed in so quickly the proprietor grew suspicious. He parted the curtains of the tent, just in time to see Father disappearing out at the back. "Collar that fella," he yelled, but was too late.

I used to stand and watch these great ferocious-looking prize fighters. They fascinated me in some ways, but frightened me as well. They looked as though they could eat little boys. And in those days I used to hear people say you had to be hungry to be a good fighter! My brother George would have liked to have had a go, but he was strongly advised not to do so.

Contingents of gypsies always turned up at fair time and camped with their large families, their dogs and vans on their

Little Holland old cottages, c. 1900.
From print owned by D. MacCarthy, Esq.

traditional spot over by Little Holland. There was always a great deal of antagonism between the fair men and the gypsies and other groups of travellers who were called gypsies whether they were or not.

There is a legend that quarrelling between gypsies and fair men reached such a pitch one day that the fair people pushed all the gypsy caravans into Clappits pond and that they are there to this day. Fighting amongst them was a regular occurrence. They would come to the fair deliberately to pay off old scores and grievances and have it out by fighting. I've heard men say, "You wait till Melford fair. I'll square you." They didn't wait long either. They'd start fighting as soon as daylight dawned on Thursday morning, before breakfast, and some of the locals would get up early especially to see the fun. Friends and relatives would form a circle and stand round urging them on. It was often very violent and very bloody and vicious and deadly serious. I used to keep out of their way. It frightened me.

Once we saw a gypsy in his pony and van chase after another gypsy also with a pony and van. They went straight down the casey at great speed and the whole lot came to grief at the rails at the bottom, breaking the shafts and collapsing on top of one another.

There were continuous fights outside the Lion and every now and then someone would be thrown out with a thump on the rough stony ground, their face all bloodied. Though I saw these things so often, they still terrified me as a child. I thought they were being killed. Usually the women stood aside and cheered on their menfolk, but I have seen women join in, specially the gypsy women, their long black hair flying and their blouses torn. Drink flowed so freely at the fair and rows were the order of the day. It was all very rough and bawdy and the language was lurid. But my grandmother told me it was far worse when she was young and she witnessed a lot of very vicious fights. She saw Mrs. Barker (the fairman's wife) come out of her tent with a gun and join in.

Grandma also remembered the Fire King or Flaming Tinman, who did a fire-swallowing act. His name was Bosville. In *Lavengro*, George Borrow tells how he fell foul of this tinman, and a young local girl named Isobel Berners came to his rescue. When Borrow was getting the worst of the fight Isobel suggested he tried the Long Melford (a heavy blow from the right arm). This proved successful and Belle joined Borrow in his journeyings. Grandma knew Isobel, who was born and brought up in the workhouse, or House of Correction, which in Grandma's early days stood next to the Black Lion in Church Row, but was demolished some time ago. She said the incident took place on the Green, near the conduit. The expression "Long Melford punch" was in use in boxing circles about this period, but I understand has since died out.

But all too soon our long-awaited fair and all its excitements came to an end. On the Friday night Mother would have great difficulty in getting us boys indoors while there was so much going on outside. But even after we were sent off to bed we would stand at the window watching all the flickering lights, and the dying glows from the braziers and the camp fires of the gypsies on the far side of the Green. The old church tower seemed to look down on the scene in a benevolent sort of way, linking all the past with the present.

Next morning the clearing up began and we boys would spend hours poking round the Green looking for any coins that may have been dropped. By Saturday night everything had to be cleared off the Green, and Sir William Parker would come round himself to make sure all was gone and was tidied up in readiness for Sunday. And peace came once more to our village. I always felt a bit sad to see them all go, but Mother and Grandmother were thankful, I know.

9

THE MAT FACTORY

We were allowed to leave school when we had reached a required standard of education, i.e. proficiency in reading, writing, grammar and arithmetic. In the year 1890 at the age of twelve I duly attained this standard and so left school. I was rather sorry on the whole as my teachers were excellent and were encouraging me in the pursuit of knowledge of all kinds, and opening up for me fresh vistas of learning.

Having no particular prospects in view, I was sent down to my mother's relatives in Norfolk to help on the farm. I hadn't been there much more than a week or so when I received an urgent message to come back post-haste as a job had been found for me at Mr. George Whittle's Mat and Matting Factory where my father, who had started work there at the age of eight, was foreman and designer. Such a wonderful opportunity couldn't be missed in those days, so home I rushed and started work the very same day as an invoice clerk.

From then on I spent many long hours perched on a high stool at a big desk struggling with large books and many figures. But I began to wonder what all the hurry was about when for the next ten weeks I received no wages at all, being classed as a learner. After this period I was paid the handsome sum of two shillings and sixpence a week, and this wage continued for a whole year. Evidently I came up to their expectations, as at the end of the year my pay was increased to five shillings a week.

Hall Street Post Office, c. 1900. Postman, Mr. Smith, talking to fiancée Miss Keeble at entrance to the Post Office. The thatched house was a butcher's shop owned by Alfred (Bodger) Allen, who is in the dog-cart. His son, Herbie, is the youth with the dog standing by the cart.
From print owned by Herbert Allen, Esq.

Before I left school I was taught the rudiments of stocks and shares and money-market dealings, and the idea that money could be invested to make more money appealed to me. Some considerable time elapsed before I was able to save up a sum which I felt could be spared for investment. It was with some pride that I finally went along to the Post Office and opened an account with two shillings. I followed the instructions printed on the book and regularly sent it up to London "to have the interest added". The book came back blank for three years running, but in the fourth year – Eureka! I'd got twopence interest! I might add, it was several more years before I was able to increase my capital.

The factory was a very busy and prosperous one, employing some 160 men and boys and a few women. They worked from six in the morning to six in the evening with Saturday afternoon and all day Sunday off, working overtime when required. The mats produced were all very well made, of excellent quality and design. The designs were done on "point paper" as there were no blueprints at that time.

The factory had branches at West Ferry Road, Milwall, London, and also at Cowley, Oxford, where many thousands of coconuts from India were delivered. At these two factories the husks were split open with old bayonets and crushed. The fibre was then combed and prepared for making up into mats. The coconuts were sold to dealers, the fibre being sent to our factory at Melford in large bales with iron hooping. Here it had to be combed again and again, ready to make into mats, and the amount of dust which came off was very considerable. This dust was excellent material for gardens and several well-known seed merchants bought truckloads from us. Local farmers also bought a lot and if anyone was seriously ill it was spread in front of the house to deaden the sound of horses' feet. So every part of the coconut was utilised to the full and even the hooping round the bales was sold to dealers.

Coco matting was made from spun yarn and this yarn mostly came from India in bales of up to two to three hundredweight. This we bought through brokers in Germany and it was despatched direct to our Melford factory. When the yarn was fully prepared it was bleached and dyed into attractive colours and the men wove thousands of hard-wearing mats. These were sold all over the United Kingdom at wholesale prices, and as far afield as Russia, Argentina, South Africa and other parts of the British Empire.

The men were all very proud of their workmanship, and I have known them work long hours to complete a special order on time. Sometimes they would come in as early as three in the morning to get an urgent job done. The key of the factory was left in a certain place well-known to the men and they would let themselves in. Most of the work was paid at piece rates and special bonuses (or boguses as the men invariably called them) were given for special or urgent jobs. We sometimes had very exceptional orders, as for example when we were asked to produce a huge mat for a circus ring, suitably dyed green of course. On the other hand we had many very modest orders, often from travelling dealers and gypsies. One regular customer who travelled the northern counties used to write regularly as follows:

"Dear sir Mr. Whittle heres 2 pounds I can trust you to send me best value for this will you send to Morpeth [or some similar destination] station to be call for yours truly ......"

We'd send him a bundle of assorted mats in various colours and sizes suitable for his itinerant trade. We supplied him for many years but never met him. I think he must have been a nice old boy.

For the period of the Melford fair the men were given two days' holiday and the factory closed down. It would hardly have been worth keeping it open in any case! On the Saturday morning the office staff would come in to serve the gypsies and other dealers as they were leaving the fair. Mr. Whittle always provided us with a cold boiled-beef dinner.

The gypsies always did a lot of business with us. There would be quite a bit of arguing as to price and they loved a bit of bargaining. We would start off by adding about two shillings a dozen to the price, knowing quite well that in the end we would get down to what was a fair price so that satisfaction was felt all round. Of course they always paid cash and we made allowance for that. Mr. Whittle got on well with the gypsies. I remember an occasion when one of them came to him and asked for the loan of fifty golden sovereigns, which he promised to return next time he came to Melford. Sure enough it was returned as promised.

Mr. Whittle, or the governor as he was popularly called, was a well-liked man, respected by his men and very easy-going. He had a little Van Dyke beard, dressed well and had an aristocratic bearing. He often visited London and Cowley in connection with his business and this enhanced his standing in the eyes of his workmen. He had a way of getting the best out of them. Neither he nor my father would order men to do a job, but in the manner of many of the old East Anglians, and especially Suffolk men, would go round the subject:

"Old so-and-so wants two dozen ...... mats by Saturday, but I doubt you could do that, Bogey?"

Thus put on his mettle the reply would come "Cors I ken. You trust me."

Or it might be "I don't suppose you could manage ......" and a quick response "That a could."

My father got on well with the matties. He had a great sense of humour and very often a quick-witted joke and a laugh would relieve a difficult situation and settle a dispute. On

Friday afternoons Father would go round the factory with a little notebook and stub of pencil recording the men's work in readiness for preparing their wage packets. Sometimes they had a mat only part-finished and would ask to be paid for it in advance. This they called "dead 'oss".

The men were paid at twelve o'clock on Saturday mornings when they left off work, and it was not an unusual sight to see three or four women waiting at the factory gate to meet their husbands to get their share of the wages before it was all spent in the pubs.

The mat-makers were a rough and ready crowd of men. Summer and winter alike they dressed in old coats and thick heavy corduroy trousers tied at the knee, their shirts open and unadorned by such falderals as collar or tie, and a cloth cap. They looked like a crowd of pirates and were known locally as "Whittle's rats". Their work was heavy and very dusty, and with beer at so cheap a price they were mostly heavy drinkers. They certainly believed in the old Suffolk saying, "You can't work on water". But in spite of much drunkenness, and also the ingrained poaching habits of a few of them, they were a fine crowd of men. They were all very good workers, conscientious and reliable. They took an immense pride in their work and would never turn out a badly finished job. They boasted to one another about their workmanship.

They were well-behaved in spite of their rough appearances and tough manners. They needed to be tough in those days when so many lived on the borderline of poverty. Several of them did other jobs to earn a bit extra, such as haircutting and trimming beards. They'd put up a barber's pole outside their houses and do it on Sunday mornings. Quite a few of them had allotments and would sell their surplus vegetables.

The careful ones did well and prospered, but it meant constant hard work.

The governor was very tolerant towards the men's heavy drinking as he knew quite well that if he needed them for some special job they would willingly help him out. One day one of the men, Bunny Piper, who was responsible for bleaching the fibre, was missing, and Mr. Whittle sent me round the pubs to look for him. In due course I ferreted him out and brought him back to the office more than half-drunk. Swaying ominously he staggered into the governor's office.

"Bunny, you're drunk."

"I'm n..n..not sir. I ain't touched a drop, sir."

"You old liar," said the governor and sent him back to his work. He had charge of a large vat of sulphuric acid for bleaching the yarn. Clear instructions were posted up as to the right amount to be used, but I'm afraid the degree of whiteness varied according to Bunny's state of intoxication at the time of mixing.

Sometimes some of the men would come in on a Monday morning after a heavy weekend and they'd work till about eleven o'clock, then go out for a livener, and more often than not stay in the pub for the rest of the day.

The governor was a generous man as well as easy-going. Sometimes if he fancied a break from work he would say to Father, "John, tell the groom to put the pony to and we'll have a drive out." The Saracen's Head at Newton Green was a favourite port of call. The governor had a large, high-spirited pony called Kitty which he used to drive back and forth from his home at Babergh Hall every day to work. Kitty was so well-fed on corn that it was a job to get her into the shafts and as soon as the stable door was opened she would shoot out like a racehorse and be up at the Saracen's Head in no time. Here they would spend the rest of the day enjoying themselves meeting farmer friends and other jovial companions, whiling away the hours till it was time to go home.

The family also had a small governess cart and a quiet and much-loved little pony called Tommy, who was almost one of the family. Tommy was used for shorter expeditions, on occasions delivering small bundles of mats to churches etc. and for the ladies' excursions. Occasionally the governor would fancy a trip to the Newmarket races and would take Father with him for an outing.

Mr. Whittle's groom, a man named Frank Snell, was a rough old diamond. He had bow legs, no doubt because of his lifetime's work with horses. He was well over seventy when I was in the office and he had a perfect set of white teeth. One day he went with some friends on an outing to the races. He had an uncanny knack of picking out the winners. "That hoss 'ull win," and sure enough it did, but he never backed any himself.

Playing practical jokes was a popular pastime in those days and Whittle's rats did their share of it in the factory. If they had a grudge against anyone they would tie a dholly of yarn and suspend it over a staircase, or perhaps a bundle of mats over a door. From this they would tie a long piece of cord to a loom some distance away. At a signal from a mate on the approach of the victim, the cord would be cut and down came the bundle. It was a dangerous trick, usually taken in good part, but occasionally the language was lurid.

There was a tremendous amount of dust in the factory, and a boy was employed especially to dampen this down and keep it swept up. I remember one day a factory inspector called (these officials were an innovation at this time and much resented by the men). This particular inspector was very officious and bumptious and very much disliked. He was standing near a large heap of dust holding forth when from the other side a pail of water was thrown with such accuracy that the inspector was soaked. He was furious. The thrower of the water came round the pile, full of profuse apologies. "I never knowed you was there sir; I swear I never did. 'Ouldn't a done it for all the world," etc. But as soon as the inspector had disappeared across the yard, his words changed dramatically, and the men roared approval of the accident.

The mat-makers were all well-known in the village, ready to help in any emergency. They were the unofficial fire-fighters for the neighbourhood. Whenever a fire occurred someone would

Coronation procession for King George V, 1911. Firemen on decorated horse-drawn fire engine still in use at this time.
Photo by E. Ambrose

come rushing into the factory shouting "Fire, Fire, Fire," and a group of the matties would drop tools immediately, never stopping to ask permission. A few would troop across the road to the back of the Bull to haul the fire appliance out, while a few more would go down the street to Fred Neave the harness-maker's shop. Here two horses were supposed to be kept in readiness in case of such emergencies, but if the animals were out on some other job it was just too bad, and they had to look elsewhere for a pair of horses. After much struggling with "ooze" pipes, as they called them, they would man the pumps. The hose pipes were never checked and I have vivid memories of as much water squirting out of the many holes in the pipes as came out of the nozzle. Before reaching this stage, however, one man would be detailed to fetch beer from the nearest pub, and it was his special job to keep the men supplied during the operation. Unfortunately, owing to the many delays caused by all these preparations, more often than not the fire won the day. Usually, after all the excitement of such an event, the rest of the day was spent in a pub talking it over. And naturally the reward for attending a fire would be an extra large supply of beer.

One day a man was leading his horse and tumbrel into the yard of Brook House next to the factory. The horse was backed over the wooden cover of a well which was in poor condition, and under the weight of the horse it collapsed. The poor animal slipped into the well and was held up only by the harness attached to the cart which stood free on one side, while the horse's forelegs clung to the side of the well. The owner never stopped to do anything himself but rushed straight into the factory yelling "Fire, Fire, Fire. Hoss down the well." About a score of matties downed tools and dashed outside and in about a quarter of an hour got the horse out with the aid of ropes. Those who had helped, as well as a few onlookers, adjourned to the Bull to celebrate the occasion at the expense of the owner of the horse and cart, and no more mat-making was done by them that day.

Another occasion I remember was when someone dashed into the factory yelling "Come quick. Boy in river." Without waiting, out ran a dozen or more men straight down to the river, where a young boy who had been missing from home for more than a week appeared to be standing upright in the middle of the river. Without hesitation one of the men jumped in and brought him out. Unfortunately he was already dead.

I suppose Bogey was one of the oldest men working in the factory. There was no old-age pension in those days and the men worked on as long as they were able (and longer too sometimes). One day Bogey had a hot argument with an equally aged workman, Picky Piper, and they both climbed out of their looms, stripped off their waistcoats and started to fight. The other men had to separate them by force.

The matties hadn't a very high opinion of each other's honesty. They were always on the make-haste themselves and expected all their pals to be the same. Bogey shot a hare before breakfast one day and because he had to go to work that morning he put it in a bag and said to his friend Jelly, "'Ere git riddy o' this fer me. Git 'arf a croon fo't. I'll see ya in the White 'art tonight." But he hadn't really any high hopes of seeing his half crown. Telling me about it the next day he said, "When I went in ta White 'art I heerd 'ole Jelly a-singin'. 'e sing like a lark when 'eve a few pints a-board. So I thought ta meself that's goodbye ta me 'alf croon. An' I didn't even git me sack back." He took it all in good part and bore no malice.

It was not an uncommon sight to see an old sack beside a loom. The sacks more often than not contained a rabbit or hare, or perhaps even a pheasant, and would pass hands unobtrusively during the course of the day.

The governor had a lot of influential friends in London and occasionally he was asked whether he could recommend a good worker who would like to try working in London. Everyone who chose to go to London to work did very well and were highly thought of by their employers. Cook's in St. Paul's Churchyard employed several of the men from our factory. One of our men went up to work in London for a few weeks, but decided to come back to the village. During his time in the great metropolis he acquired a bit of a cockney accent and to show off his superiority he tried to "talk proper" when he got back home. He was promptly nicknamed "La-de-da" by his mates and always baited about his life in the big city.

The daughter of one of the mat-makers went to work in service in London. When she came back for a holiday her father met her at the station. She opened the carriage door with a flourish, and standing on the high step in her smart London clothes, said in what she thought was a refined manner aping her mistress, "How does Father does? and how does Mother does? and how does all the little ones?" But Father was not at all impressed and told his daughter in no polite terms, "Come down, you does-y dav'l. You'll keep on does-ing all day."

As I have said, the men got on very well with Mr. Whittle. They liked the old man even though he swore at them at times and said they'd ruin him. He worked in with them and they felt they had a share in the running of the business. In the summer trade often got rather slack, and when this happened some of them would ask the governor if they could "take a harvest".

Most of them could scythe and load and they would make a bargain with a farmer for about £6 or £7 each to "do the harvest", according to the acreage.

Usually a group of eight or nine men would get together for this work and one of them would be appointed leader or "Lord of the harvest". He thought himself a mighty important person as he would be boss of the team and lead in the cutting of the corn. "When I stops fer a rub, they all 'as ter stop. And when I sturts agin they all 'as ter sturt agin."

Harvest field, c. 1910. Boy on horse Alfred Woodgate; second from right: Alfred Bulmer; third right: Tom Woodgate; holding wagon shaft: Jim Sansum.
Photo by E. Ambrose

They all felt great pride in getting the harvest done in good time and would boast of their achievements. If the weather was wet it might take up to six or seven weeks, but in a dry spell they could do it in about three. As it was a contract they received their agreed sum however long it took.

Then came the celebrations and these were royal occasions, what with the horkeys in the pubs and barns, and the harvest festivals in the churches. The men's harvest money usually meant a trip down to Sudbury to fit the family out with boots and warm clothing for the winter. Some would put their money aside for the year's rent, but many of them thought they were millionaires for a week or two and had a grand time treating their mates and living it up high till they were back on the rocks again.

The railways at this time used to advertise cheap day excursions to London for about five shillings or less return, and one of the matties, Snowy Allen, who'd never travelled by train before, decided he'd give himself a treat, so he went up one Saturday. On the Monday following this exciting outing the men gathered round, keen to hear how he'd got on in the great city.

"I had a wonderful time. It were lovely."

"What did you do, Snowy? What did you see?"

"When I got to Liverpool Street I went into the first pub. I came across. It were beautiful, all decorated and smart. The best pub. I've iver seen. Then some fellers came in and they kep' on treating me, asking about the country where I come from. Then treating me agin and agin. It were lovely. An' I stayed there till it were time to come 'oom."

This adventure encouraged others to take the trip. I remember one who had a good time in London, though he went a little further afield than Snowy. On his way back to Liverpool Street he developed a nasty pain. A man said to him, "Don't you feel well?" And he said, "No, I want to go somewhere." So he directed him down some steps and explained that he had to put a penny in a slot and pull a chain afterwards. The mattie went on to say, "An' I did what he told me, and it were marvellous, and then when it stopped roaring there was enough water left in when it were finished ta wash ya 'ands an' face if you was a-minded to!"

I can still recall the day when I first encountered a water closet myself. I think it was on a visit to London. On pulling the attachment I thought the whole contraption was coming down over my head. It frightened me. I thought I had done some damage, as the machinery made such an unearthly roar and clatter. But when I thought of the stinking pits and buckets which served our purpose in Melford, I agreed with our friend, and thought the new-fangled water closets were indeed marvellous!

I remember another mat-maker, Shonk Pleasants, who decided to have a day's trip to London. Fearing they might not get anything to eat in the great metropolis he got his wife to pack a bag with a good supply of home-made wine and cake. On arrival at Mark's Tey the train was shunted back and in alarm he said, "Missus, they're a-takin' on us back 'oom. Well let's eat the grub anyway." And they quickly ate the lot. But as Shonk said afterwards, "We was took ta London arter all."

There were always a lot of animals about in those pre-motor days. Most of the mat-makers had dogs who would follow them to work, and you would usually see a few hanging round waiting for their masters to come out again. They'd follow them to the pubs, too, and you could very often tell the whereabouts of a man by the dogs waiting outside.

Our engineer, Poulter Whittle, who lived in the cottage next to the Bull, opposite the factory, made a habit of feeding his chickens as soon as he went home to dinner at one o'clock prompt. He was so prompt in fact that at five to one the chickens would regularly come wandering across the wide road looking for him. We always knew what time it was when we saw Poulter's chickens in the road.

The Bull was always a very busy house and was used a lot by commercial travellers. One regular customer, a man named Fountain, was a fine-looking old man, with beautiful white hair and stiff side-whiskers. He dressed very smartly and had a military appearance as he marched along with his swinging cane and tall top hat. He came out of the Bull promptly at five to two on a certain day every week. At this time the matties would be standing at the corner of the lane waiting for the factory bell to ring for start of work again at two o'clock. As soon as they caught sight of the old man emerging from the Bull they would start whistling a lively military tune. I can still recall the lilting air. It obviously pleased the old man. He marched along and raised his hat in salute to the men across the road, smiling benignly. Then he went on his way to make his weekly call at Wickham's grocery shop in Hall Street.

A retired judge lived at Brook House, next door to the factory, and the men used to gather close to his house while waiting for the bell to ring for them to go in to work. He was so impressed by the men's good behaviour that at Christmas time he always presented them with a quarter of a pound of tobacco each. It was some of the best bacca on the market, Poole's Derby Mixture. He sent away to Derby specially for this. This gesture pleased the men tremendously and made for good relationships. One of the men, who didn't smoke, sold his to me for sixpence, the current market price. This was my first attempt at smoking, and I am afraid I have continued the practice to this day.

We used to have very lively election meetings when I was young and though I was not very knowledgeable on the subject I used to enjoy listening to the arguments. Sir W. Cuthbert Quilter was M.P. for many years and I believe was well-liked. The sports ground at Sudbury was bought largely due to the generosity of Sir Cuthbert. I remember he had six very fine shire horses and they were used in the Lord Mayor's show in London one year. He had also a very proud and pompous coachman who sat up on his box, whip in hand, looking as if he owned the lot, though I wouldn't mind betting he only got twelve shillings and sixpence a week wages.

Electioneering meetings were often held near the factory gates and the mat-makers would stand around listening. The men knew far more about local conditions than did many of the prospective candidates and their spokesmen, but they couldn't express themselves, and in those days if a lower dog gave an opinion he was promptly sat on.

I was very amused on one occasion when the Rev. Packer from Hartest came to address the matties on politics. He was a local magistrate and in that capacity had fined or jailed quite a few of the matties for poaching. The meeting got a bit rowdy and he was shouted down. In great annoyance he roared back, "Working men of Long Melford, I will be heard." But the matties shouted back, "You 'ont you old bugger. We 'ave ta listen ta you on the bench; now you listen to we."

When the Liberals came along and expounded their policies with the slogan "Three acres and a cow", and more especially their Free Trade plans, the matties muttered, "It's orl right fer the likes of you, but it 'ont do for the likes of we." It meant foreign mats coming into the country and being sold cheaply, while our mat-makers went on short time through lack of orders. This ultimately caused the final closing down of the factory, but that came much later on.

When a party of Kensit's anti-popery followers visited Melford, the mat-makers were swift to take action. They set up their wagon in Hall Street and, preaching blood and fire, threatened to break down the church ornaments. The headmaster of the village school, Mr. Whitehead, gathered a group of people to oppose them. He was vigorously assisted by a vociferous group of mat-makers (who probably never entered the church). They were so incensed at the thought of their village church being desecrated that they threatened to turn over the wagon, and the anti-popery party had to retire quickly in disarray, thanks to the help of the mat-makers.

On Easter Tuesday, 27 March 1894, the last meeting of the old Board of Guardians was held in the vestry, presided over by the Rev. G. St. John Topham. From a newspaper report of this meeting it appears there was some confusion about the appointment of Overseers in the new Parish Councils to be formed, and Mr. C.J.N. Row raised the question.

Chairman: "Have you seen the Act, Mr. Row?"
Mr. Row: "Yes."
Chairman: "Well, how do you read it?"
Mr. Row: "I think it would want a double lawyer knocked into one to understand it. Certainly it can't be understood by ordinary mortals like myself."
Chairman: "It is very difficult to understand."

However in the eyes of the villagers and especially the mat-makers the sooner they got rid of the "Gardeens" – and the Overseers too – the better, and great was the enthusiasm for the formation of the new Parish Council. Noisy meetings were held and a large number of people were persuaded to put up for election, eager to get on the first Parish Council. The most popular people in the village were elected, but after they'd had three years of it most of them said "Let someone else have a go!" My father was on this first Council.

Another stirring period in the life of the village was the introduction of gas for street lighting. The arguments for and against and the many rowdy meetings on the subject went on for many months, in fact for two or three years. A leaflet was circulated entitled "Six reasons why the Ratepayers of Melford should not have a Rate forced on them for Lighting up the Streets". Three of the reasons given were:

Because the School Rate and Gas Rate will raise the
    Poor man's cottage Rent.
Because the old inhabitants in Melford Street can be
    led but not easily driven.
Because we must pay a Rate for the Road, and a Rate
    for the Schools, and a Rate for the Poor, which is
    quite enough for Melford.

Many of the villagers and all the mat-makers were against it and loudly proclaimed their opinions. A subscription list was opened and gifts ranging from sixpence to £3 3s 0d were contributed. It was kept open for three years, by which time the total was £138 9s 0d. Mr. C.J.N. Row, who was the chief instigator of the scheme, had guaranteed £150 for the three years, so he gave the £11 11s 0d to complete the sum.

From our office window at the factory we often saw groups of people near the Bull arguing and even coming to blows about the gas. Mr. William Richold, the brush-maker, who lived at Walnuttree House (now next to the Bull) was furiously opposed to it, and one morning we were amazed to see GAS in two-foot-high letters daubed in tar on each side of his front door. Someone tried to clean it off but it still showed through after very many years.

10

More about Bogey and his Poaching Friends

Poaching was regarded as a sport and a regular way of life. Among the mat-makers were some of the finest exponents of this game. They were persistent and irrepressible in spite of the heavy and often harsh penalties if they were caught. Bogey Tebble (Suffolk pronunciation of Theobald) was one of the best. He was a smallish chap, with a billy-goat beard and screwed-up face. He had sharp features and was very quick-witted, tough and bent through hard work. He was a man of about sixty when I started at the factory and he was fond of telling me, with a chuckle, of how he had so often outwitted the gamekeepers and the police. It was his one aim and object and he thoroughly enjoyed it. We used to read him bits out of the newspaper of where the criminal got away and the police were outwitted. This highly delighted him. "Good ol' bor," he'd say.

In his early days (around the 1860s) he had served two terms of imprisonment of one month each. He told me of the horrible conditions in the prison, of the skilly (thin watery porridge) he was given and the shortage of food. He said if a bird flew over the prison yard and dropped a piece of bread prisoners would make a dive for it. He told me of the rough treatment by the warders and of how he had to work on a treadmill, where he had to hold on to a rail above his head and keep on treading on steps like a perpetual moving staircase. Apparently this treadmill was invented by Mr. Orridge (one time governor of Bury St. Edmunds prison) who thought the exercise would be good for prisoners' health as well as their morals! He got an engineer named Mr. Cubitt of Ipswich to make the machine and it was erected in prisons all over the United Kingdom. It was nicknamed Cubitt's anti-rheumatic wheel.

Despite this experience in prison, as soon as Bogey got out he went straight back to poaching. He was a rare character and had a marvellous sense of humour. I would imagine one needed this attribute to be a successful poacher. Describing a visit one dark night to the hen house of a local farmer he said, "Me an' my ole pal Jelly, we jes' got ta door of 'en 'ouse when we heerd Wch—Wch—Wch, like ol' 'ens goo when they be disturbed. Ol' Jelly 'e say 'Doan' matter which. You've all gotta coom.'" And he put the lot in his bag.

Another night some poachers visited Mr. Wright's farm at Preston, near Lavenham, where six geese and a gander were kept. Taking a sack with them they cautiously approached the farmyard and successfully stole the geese. They tied a crude note to the neck of the gander, reading:

Mr. Rite we bid you goodnite
Tis time for we to wander
Weve bort yor geese
For a penny a pece
And left the mony with the gander.

103

They attached an envelope in which they placed six pennies.

A young man was very keen to join the poaching community and they decided to give him a trial.

"You coom along a we. We'll learn ya."

In due course he went and some days later I heard the outcome of the first expedition. The new boy was told explicitly to take up his position near a gate and keep watch on a footpath. If by any chance anyone came along he was to bash him on the head with a big stick.

"Don't ask no questions and don't make no noise, just bash 'im."

The new boy duly laid in wait and kept silent. Suddenly someone came running along the path. It was a foggy morning and he couldn't see who it was, but remembering his strict instructions he bashed the intruder and laid him out. Suddenly he realised his mistake and was horrified.

"Is that you, Jelly? I'm terrible sorry."

"Thet's orl rite, bor. You done what we told ya."

Another young man didn't come off quite so well. He asked to join the poaching fraternity and was duly instructed in the art of setting snares. One night he was sent out to set snares, told exactly where to go and left to do the job himself. Suddenly two men in gamekeepers' clothes pounced on him.

"Ah, we've got ya. Red 'anded too."

The boy was terrified and instantly blamed his friends. "It was Mr...... and Mr....... wot telled me to do it. It wasn't me."

"You bugger" was the polite reply he got, "so that's the sort of man you are."

And they promptly gave him a good hiding. The "keepers" turned out to be two of his instructors who had borrowed gamekeepers' jackets from the landlord of a pub, a retired keeper himself, and who, incidentally, fully enjoyed the joke.

The poachers loved to outwit the gamekeepers and spent their lives scheming how to get the better of them, enjoying nothing better than to bait them on their own grounds. The inns were of course favourite places for these encounters and the Hare in particular was popular because of its position opposite Kentwell gates. I always enjoyed these witty encounters, and I can still see in my mind the group of keepers sitting there in the smoke room. I specially remember Squinks Ford and Bill Fakes. One evening one of the poachers came in carrying a beautiful fully grown hare. There sat the keepers, looking glum. He held the animal up high for all to admire, and stroking its beautiful fur, said, "There nar. Ain't 'e a beauty?", and turning to the keepers added, "D'yew think that coom orf ya bit?"

Bogey told me one morning how he had that day met our village policeman, a man named Grimwood. He'd got his single-barrelled muzzle-loader gun tucked under his arm, and in it was only one charge.

"Mornin' Mr. Tebble," said Grimwood.

"Mornin'."

"Decent gun you got there?"

"Ain't bad.'"

"Ken I 'av a look at it?"

The policeman took it, aimed at a small bush and blew the top off. "What were you gooing ta use thet for?"

"Only rooks."

"Tidy strong charge fer rooks, weren't it?"

What Bogey thought of the policeman and his action was beyond description.

Some of the matties would take their guns to work with them. They'd tuck them under the loom and cover them with fibre. The governor knew about it, but made no objections. You could almost always get a brace of rabbits for a few pence.

Bogey told me that some of his pals were sentenced to a month each by a Melford magistrate as a result of evidence given against them. They swore to have their revenge on this hated informer when they came out of prison, and they went to a lot of trouble to carry out their plan. Some neighbour had occasion to kill a goat and they obtained a quantity of the blood, which they put in a pail. Late one night one of the men carried this pail of blood and a garden syringe while his pal took a gun. They knocked on the door of the house and the occupant threw open the bedroom window and looked out. The gun was shot into the air and at the same moment a syringe full of goat's blood was squirted very accurately all over his nightshirt. He yelled out in alarm, "Missus, they've shot me!" and promptly collapsed with shock.

Old Bogey Tebble had an uncle who was well-known in the district as a very successful rat-catcher. He was a tough character with fine rugged features. An artist, Mr. G.S. Ffitch, painted a portrait in oils of the old man in 1840, and the picture was hung on a back staircase at Melford Hall. This old man used to imbibe freely and was usually in a state of semi-intoxication, but this in no way impaired his sharp intellect and ready tongue.

One evening Bogey and some of his pals thought they'd try to scare the old gentleman. They each procured a large white sheet and draped them over their arms and waited for the old boy to come out of the White Hart in his usual state of inebriation. At last he emerged and they paraded about twenty yards or so in front of him. He pulled up in surprise. "What ...a ghost... I've niver sin one o' they afore. I'll see what you're

Theobald the rat-catcher. Portrait painted by G.S. Ffitch in 1840.
By courtesy of Sir Richard Hyde Parker, Bt

a-made on. I'll git me gun." And off he went to get it. But on
his return the ghosts had disappeared. They knew all too well
he'd carry out his threat, and he was a deadly shot.

Bogey told me that when he was a young man there used to be
cock-fighting and bare-fisted prize-fighting on Melford Green,
but the police got too hot for them. When this happened they
used to walk from Melford to Cockfield Green and hold these
contests in a meadow at the back of the Greyhound. They'd
start out before daybreak and get there just at dawn. Among

the spectators would be a few top-hatted gentry, half disguised in heavy clothes. In fact they were often the promoters, and they would drive over to the fights. There was always a lot of betting and often the stakes were high. The fights were often brutal and bloodthirsty, the supporters urging their champions on to the extreme point of exhaustion. I know we had some very good prize-fighters in the village when I was a boy, but I never had anything to do with these fights myself, though I have a suspicion that my father may have done.

Bogey reckoned he had the gift of curing warts (for a financial consideration of course) and he practised his art whenever he could find a willing patient. A servant girl at Borley Rectory had both her hands badly covered with warts and Bogey asked her how many she had and then offered to cure them. "They'll goo," he said. A few weeks later the girl sent Bogey a message by me to say they hadn't gone, but she thanked him all the same for trying, and sent him two shillings in an envelope. At first he brushed it aside, then realising there really was two shillings inside he said, "Ah, the dear good mawther. But she couldn't a counted 'em proper do they'd all a gone."

One day Bogey saw one of his workmates with a huge wart on his hand.

"You've got a rare ol' wart thar ain't ya? It'll goo."

Later on he met the man again and enquiring about the wart was told it had gone "thank you very much".

"Is that all?" said Bogey (quite expecting a tip).

"Yes," said the man.

"Well I 'ope one'll coom on ya face then."

And strangely enough one did come on his face.

II

RECREATIONS

Many people at this period were far too occupied toiling and moiling for long hours trying to make ends meet to have much time for leisure; but those of us who could got great pleasure out of very simple things. In winter, which always seemed to be more wintry than it is now, skating was a very popular sport and parties of us would walk down to Brundon meadows to perform on the frozen fields and display our skills or otherwise on the ice. The favourite meadow was at the corner of Melford Road and Brundon Lane. For the price of sixpence you could hire a pair of skates and even have an attendant to fix them on for you. As darkness fell, the meadow was illuminated by flaming torches and it was great fun to see the performances on the frozen field.

In our own homes we made our own amusements, giving hilarious parties and concerts. "You come and have a cup of tea along-a we next Sat'day," and this would more often than not develop into an impromptu concert or a musical evening. Most of the middle-class families had a piano of some sort and it was a great asset if a member of the family could perform thereon. A "lovely touch" on the piano was much admired. It was a great help too if one or two members could sing, and if they could produce a slight tremble in the voice, that added charm to the popular sentimental ballads of the day. Duets and trios were in great demand and most of us had a go at this.

Dancing too was a popular pastime. A group of us joined Miss Pepper's quadrille class at Sudbury. This was quite a high-class establishment. Miss Pepper was very strict and proper and we had to behave ourselves with dignity and decorum. She taught us the graceful set dances such as the lancers and quadrilles.

The highlights of the season were the public and private dances. These were held at the Four Swans or Town Hall, or perhaps at Victoria Hall, and were grand occasions with full evening dress being worn. The young ladies' dresses were very lovely, of beautiful colours and material and very voluminous. They usually made their own dresses, and great care and much talk accompanied the preparations, which went on for many days before these events took place. Our engagement cards had twenty-four dances on them and Miss Pepper saw to it that no gentleman sat out if a lady was not dancing, so we were kept hard at it.

The Melford ladies would usually drive down in their own carriages, while a party of us boys and men would hire the wagonette from the Bull, called Why Not. It held sixteen people and anyone could hire it, together with a fine pair of horses, for quite a small sum. There was considerable rivalry between Melford and Sudbury and even at these prim and proper dances this sometimes came to the surface, the cause usually being a young lady. I have known times when verbal threats have been heard above the genteel talk, and friends have had to "persuade" companions to desist from using fisticuffs.

I still have vivid memories of the servants' balls, especially those given at Kentwell Hall. They were splendid occasions. Sir John and Lady Aird would come out and take the lead in dancing and then retire. The refreshments were specially sought after; they were always sumptuous and included champagne. It was on one of these occasions that jelly was introduced, "that 'ere shaky stuff". It was a great novelty at the time, causing much hilarity. Sometimes I was invited to play for these dances and was always treated royally by the butler and the family too.

On one occasion when I was invited to play, a well-known character in the village, Tom Salter, turned up clutching to his chest a brand new pair of dancing slippers. Before dancing even commenced he had refreshed himself with three or four drinks of whisky (his favourite beverage), and by the third dance he was all over the place. The butler came to me at a loss to know what to do with him. We decided to appoint him M.C. in the hope it might sober him up.

"What's that?" says Tom.

"Well you have to announce the dances."

So he came and asked me what the next dance was to be and I told him a schottische. Tom gave out:

"Ladies an' gentl'ming the next dance is a sch...sch... schottischer-er-er."

And then retired to have a few more of his favourite drinks. Towards midnight it was decided to get the brougham out and take Tom home.

We had another jolly evening at a dance at Shimpling School. Sixteen of us went, boys and girls, all in full evening dress. We hired the wagonette and horses from the Bull. The manager of the Bull, Fred Achurch, a friend of mine, said that, as no intoxicants were allowed on the school premises, he would take half a gallon of whisky with us, and get a friend in a nearby cottage to take charge of it.

The food was arranged in the Infants' room. A large sheet was spread over some of the forms and the plates of pies and cakes etc. were put on the forms. At half time we all went for refreshments and you can imagine the dodging backwards and forwards between the cottage for the whisky and the school for the food. In the confusion someone stumbled and fell on a corner of the sheet and down came all the tarts and cakes in one glorious mess.

We saw to it that the band had plenty of refreshments, especially of the liquid variety, and lushed them up generously with the whisky. When we went back for the second half there was a most extraordinary exhibition from the band. There was Shad Frost, the pianist, running up and down the keyboard producing all sorts of sounds at an increasing tempo. Crick Moore, the grocer, was floundering on his double bass, fishing for notes, and Sherriff Long, the schoolmaster, was doing his best on his violin to search for a dance tune. It was a hilarious evening, and everyone was highly delighted, and took it all as a great joke.

I am afraid lushing up the band was a popular thing to do. When I was playing for a dance I tried to be careful, but it was thirsty work and hard work too. On more than one occasion I was given a bottle for my own consumption, which was stowed away behind the piano and brought out for a nip when so inclined.

Holidays were not thought of when I was a boy, so a day's outing was a long remembered event. One day my father and his friend Mr. Reynolds thought they'd like to arrange a family outing to see the gardens at Hardwick House, Bury. Mr. Byford, who had a large carrier's van or dray, lent it to them for the occasion. The van could be covered but we had it open as it was such a lovely warm summer's day. There were about ten adults and the same number of children. A form and some chairs were placed along each side of the van to provide seating and we all climbed in. We had to economise, not having much money, so we took our own refreshments with us, a good supply of cakes and pies supplied by the ladies, and a nice quantity of home-made beer. A heavy and very strong horse pulled us all the way to Bury, and it took a little over two hours. This gave us time to enjoy the scenery and to observe the conditions of the crops and notice the few cottage gardens, as well as to greet other travellers on the road. It was a grand drive and all the more fun when we had to hold on to each other as the big van lurched and swayed over the uneven and rough road.

On arrival at the lovely grounds the old horse was let out to graze and the van became our hotel. Beer was passed round, which we much appreciated, as it was a dusty ride. We walked round the beautiful gardens and specially admired the splendid greenhouses, where oranges, limes and lemons were grown. Then we tucked into our food and it tasted very good indeed in such lovely surroundings. The children played a few games while the adults just admired the scenery, before we set off home again. It was a lovely outing and I can still recall a sense of blissful happiness it gave us. I was about fourteen years old, so it must have been about eighty years ago.

About this time we began to taste fresh delights at our parties with the introduction of the talking machine, called a phonograph, designed by Edison Bell. A cylindrical record was placed on a machine, the motor wound up and set going, and strains of a song came over the air in a scratchy nasal voice. This caused tremendous excitement. After a while we were able to buy blank cylinders for about a shilling or less and made our own recordings and this created even greater amusement at our parties.

This was a time of much inventiveness and we all tried to have a go at something new. It was a time of primitive films, animated pictures or living pictures as they were called. All sorts of weird streaks obliterated the image, but if we occasionally got glimpses of what it was all about we felt we'd had our money's worth.

Cameras began to be developed. My first one was made out of a wooden Colman's mustard box which I got from the grocer and a nine-penny lens. The glass plates we used cost a penny a time. We had very varied results and there were many failures, but we persevered and gradually improved on our home-made efforts.

QUEEN VICTORIA'S JUBILEE AND THE NEW CHURCH TOWER

Queen Victoria's diamond jubilee was celebrated on 22 June 1897 and the villagers went to a lot of trouble to mark the occasion in a fitting manner. Flags and bunting were unearthed from attics and the streets and houses decorated. Photos of the good queen, in varying states of preservation, were displayed to show the loyalty of her subjects. Bean feasts and parties were held and much enjoyed by all and sundry. The sun shone bright all day long, people remarked "Queen's weather", and her message was read wherever possible: "From my heart I thank my beloved people. May God bless them." And we all felt very patriotic and very contented.

Whittle's rats did their share in providing entertainment both for themselves and for the villagers. At our Cowley factory there were six ancient six-pounder guns. They belonged to J.H. Vavasseur from whom we rented the premises. The governor got two of these down to Melford. About a dozen or so of the mat-makers dressed up as sailors with straw hats and long ribbons and baggy trousers. They processed through Melford streets dragging these guns on a small timber jim with a long shaft attached, accompanied by crowds of small children and other followers. Finally they pulled one of the guns up to the school meadows and placed it facing the church, with the intention of firing a royal salute.

A hole was dug in the ground and the shaft inserted. No one had any knowledge at all as to the correct way of using this ancient weapon, but nothing daunted, they filled the muzzle with an unknown quantity of gunpowder, stuffed it tight with paper, attached a fuse and retiring to a discreet distance, ignited it. The report was tremendous and builders working on the church roof said they felt the vibrations.

After the smoke had died down, the patriotic matties inspected their handiwork. They had forgotten to allow for the rebound and the muzzle had been flung up into the air and the shaft broken. But they were highly delighted with their effort and pronounced it "Werry good". And as one of the matties said, "It wholly wollied" (vollied).

For our evening's entertainment we had a high old time on the Green. A huge bonfire had been built in front of Bixby's bakehouse. It was thirty feet high and had been carefully erected by Mr. Crowfoot, an architect. It was a great success and the merry-making lasted well into the night, the pub especially having a record turnover.

Sudbury celebrated the occasion in a more sophisticated manner. They organised a fancy dress ball which was given in the Drill Hall under the auspices of the mayor, Mr. A. Grimwood. This was described in a local newspaper as a "colourful and well-attended spectacular", but I never heard tell whether any of our locals were present on this splendid occasion.

After the great upsurge of patriotism evoked by Queen

Victoria's diamond jubilee and the imminence of the new century, the leaders of the church began to feel it would be a good opportunity to have some fitting memorial of these two outstanding occasions. The Rev. G. St. John Topham, who was now rector, suggested the raising of the church tower to bring it more in harmony with the beauty and size of the main building. This suggestion was quickly taken up with much enthusiasm and a committee was formed in 1897 to raise funds and to appoint an architect for the purpose. The original tower had been destroyed by lightning about the year 1710 and had been replaced by a square red brick tower covered with cement, which had in many places broken away and was very ugly.

The architect appointed was Mr. George F. Bodley and the builders were Messrs. Rattee and Kett of Cambridge. It was decided to build on to the brick tower rather than pull it down; and to chip off the old cement, replacing it with decorative flint-work and stones, adding buttresses at the corners faced with stone work, thus giving the tower a new though ancient look in keeping with the fifteenth-century church. Several Melford workmen were engaged for the re-building, among them William Griss, nicknamed Schemer Griss, an expert bricklayer and a man who took very great pride in his work. Mr. Griss had the honour of laying the first brick of the new foundation in 1898. Special hardstone was delivered to the church, brought there in great blocks by horse and wagon. So also were the flints which were dug out of the gravel pits at Acton. An awning was set up near the church porch and here the stonemasons cut their stone according to their needs, and flint knappers from Brandon prepared flints to fit in with delicate accuracy.

The head stonemason, a clever craftsman who came from Cambridge, used to lodge during the week with my grandmother, and we became very friendly during the three years he spent on the work. He was very appreciative of Grandma's cooking, especially her pies! I watched him at work many times and was most interested.

The ceremony of the laying of the foundation cornerstone on 10 April 1899 was a very impressive occasion. As the Freemasons had contributed so generously to the funds, they were chiefly responsible for the service. A Masonic Lodge was held in the village school before proceeding up the Green for the ceremony. The Rev. C.J. Martyn, our former rector, who, as well as being Chaplain in Ordinary to the Queen, was Deputy Provincial Grand Master of Suffolk and Past Grand Chaplain of England, conducted the service and ceremony. Underneath the stone were placed a specimen of each coin in use at that time.

In 1900 a further appeal had to be made as funds were running low and a second contract was made with the builders to raise the tower to include a ringing chamber, roof, gutters, etc. In October 1902 the Rev. Topham resigned through ill-health, and work was suspended during the winter months. In March 1903 a further contract was made with the builders and work resumed, which included additions to the battlements and pinnacles and extension of the circular staircase to the tower. In memory of the (now) late Queen Victoria and the accession of King Edward VII and Queen Alexandra, the four new pinnacles were named Victoria, Edward, Alexandra and Martyn. On 14 October 1903 the new tower (now 118 feet in height) was dedicated by the Lord Bishop of Ely.

Two of the pinnacles from the old tower went to Melford

Hall. The other two were placed on the gates at Kentwell Hall. However one of these was later retrieved from the old rectory garden, and the fourth one was bought by Sir Richard Hyde Parker at the Kentwell Hall sale in 1970. So the four pinnacles are now in the grounds of Melford Hall.

13

ORGANS AND CHOIRS

My study of the organ continued under the expert tuition of Mr. Bernard Hurst (one of five brothers, all organists) until, at the age of eighteen, I was invited to become organist at the little church at Borley. I used to cycle over every Friday evening for choir practice and again on Sundays for services. If the roads were very bad or too deep in snow, I would walk, taking short cuts across fields. I'd always arrange to arrive about half an hour before the service and would often stand on the hill looking down towards Melford. It was interesting to watch the people coming from Rodbridge making their way to the church over the stile, and diagonally across the field and then alongside the hedge. Most especially was it fascinating on dark nights when groups of worshippers carried lanterns and you would see these little lights bobbing along like fire-flies as the people made their way to church.

It was a very well-attended church and we had an enthusiastic choir. In winter we had "evening service" at three o'clock in the afternoon. I was always invited to stay to lunch at the rectory, and on arrival before morning service was given a glass of beer, which was very welcome after my efforts to get there.

The Rev. Harry Bull was rector at that period and I got to

know the family well. I began to hear about their ghost, which the family spoke about in quite matter-of-fact terms. The rector's sisters seemed mostly concerned with this apparition and when I asked them about it they told me in quite casual terms what they had seen. They pointed out to me the path and lawn where they had seen the ghost walking, and when I asked what they felt about it, they said, "Oh, we are quite used to it. It doesn't bother us at all." They also showed me a bedroom window where it appeared during the last week in July. That made me think it could be due in some way to the special position of the sun at that time. They were all very down-to-earth women, not given to exaggeration or emotionalism; nor were they inclined to search for the supernatural. But they were very convinced that they had seen an apparition on several occasions, and they just accepted this as a plain fact. They were very practical women, and if, as happened occasionally, I got a puncture in my bike, one of them would mend it for me and enjoy doing it.

A young housemaid, who had only been at the rectory a short time and had heard no talk of ghosts, told me she came home one evening and in the semi-darkness saw a person dressed as a nun or nurse standing at the lower garden gate. She approached it and it vanished. She was so terrified she fainted.

One summer's evening the Rev. Bull, who also was a pragmatic type of man, told me he was standing in the church talking to a friend (I had just left after the service) when they both distinctly heard knocking outside starting from the south side and continuing the whole way round the church. On investigation they found nothing.

I was organist at Borley for seventeen years and often left after choir practice on dark nights, but I saw nothing at all. I am by no means psychic and if I encounter an unusual situation I always seek, and usually find, a natural explanation. Ghosts and house haunts were, however, often talked of and believed in when I was a boy. People believed explicitly in evil spirits and in apparitions and most certainly in the devil. Children were often threatened with the devil: "You marn't do that do the dev'l get ya." Spirits of good and evil were considered a natural part of everyday life; and heaven and hell were very real places in the minds of ordinary people.

Bernard Hurst was often invited to give organ recitals in the neighbourhood and as by now many of us had acquired bicycles of some sort or another we felt freer to go further afield. On one occasion Bernard went to give a recital at St. James's Church, Bury St. Edmunds, and he asked Tom Wickham and me to go with him. We cycled there on the very bad roads. It was hard going and took us nearly two hours. Bernard gave an excellent performance, after which we were invited to a generous supper at the Dog and Partridge before our return journey. Our newly acquired cycles gave us some trouble on our way home, first one breaking down, then another. The roads were very bad in daylight, but it was far worse at night. However we finally reached Melford a little after two in the morning.

On another occasion Bernard and I cycled to Ipswich to hear Sir Walter Parratt, a well-known London organist, who came to open a new organ at the Social Settlement there. We thoroughly enjoyed the recital, after which we adjourned to have a meal at the Golden Lion. When we came out to go home there was a heavy rainstorm. We dared not risk cycling in those conditions, especially in the dark, so we stayed the night at the hotel. It was quite an adventure to go cycling at that time; in fact it was far easier to walk than to cycle.

On St. Peter's Day, 29 June 1911, Bernard and I were invited to attend the dedication of the new organ at St. Peter's, Sudbury. It is a very fine organ with three manuals and fifty-seven draw stops, the specification of which was drawn up by Mr. E.E. Vinnicombe, Dr. W. Inglis Mason and Mr. Thomas Elliston. An excellent recital was given by Dr. Mann, organist at King's College, Cambridge. After the evening service Dr. Mason invited Mr. Vinnicombe, Bernard and me and a few other organists to a drink at the Freemasons Hotel, where we had a very jolly convivial evening together. We enjoyed ourselves so much that it was midnight before we broke up the happy party. When we got out into the fresh air we found it was not very easy – indeed it was impossible – to mount our cycles, and Bernard, in his customary polite manner said, "My dear friend, I think we will walk a little." And with varying degrees of steadiness we walked along the Melford Road. It was not until we reached Abbey Road that Bernard said, "Do you think we might try to mount again now?" With some uncertainty we managed and so finally reached home again.

Bernard was walking home from Lavenham one night after playing for some service when halfway he passed a big gypsy encampment. The road was very bad indeed just there, having recently had a lot of flints put down. Presently he heard footsteps following him and sensed the gypsies were behind him. He stopped and they stopped. This happened two or three times, but finally they realised he knew they were following him and they turned back. He was a strong man and could have given them a very good account of himself. On another night he was walking home from Cavendish, where he had been playing, when near the Three Tuns at Glemsford he was accosted by two roughs. He knocked one out and the other made off as quickly as he could.

I continued as organist at Borley until the outbreak of war, when I was mobilised. In 1916 I was sent to France where I used to play the piano with the Fife and Drum Band of the Bedfordshire Regiment when out of the lines. We had some fine concerts and very nice services in a large cinema hut which the men enjoyed. Our CO, Col. Collins-Wells, was very fond of music and did everything he could to encourage the band.

One day the Colonel sent for me and asked my age (I was nearly forty). He said, "You've been out here fifteen months without leave and I've decided to send you to Calais for a week's rest. I'm expecting very important things to happen here very soon and you may never get back to the regiment. Should this happen I wish you good luck," and he shook my hand. Two days after I left, the final German push started. My cookhouse was completely destroyed and the transport depot captured. There were very heavy casualties among the men I had worked with and the Colonel lost his life. He was posthumously awarded the VC. The action of the Colonel in sending me on leave saved my life, I believe. After a medical I was put in a reserve battalion and moved from place to place.

One lovely summer's afternoon we marched into a ruined village called Fleurbaix near Agincourt. In the evening I went for a walk on my own to find the parish church. It was a wonderfully beautiful moonlight night and the ruins of the church stood out in stark contrast. The horrors of war pressed heavily on me as I saw all the symbols of the church shattered to pieces at my feet. As I stood there it suddenly came to me I had seen it all before, and I recalled a very vivid dream I had had as a young man. From the ruins I picked up a piece of stained glass. It was of an apple surrounded by leaves. From another ruined church at Balluel I brought home a piece of red glass, and together they made a nice set. They were placed in a window in the chancel over the organ at Melford church, but later on the whole window was taken out.

One summer's evening towards the end of the war I took a walk with a friend to a small village and we came to the little church at a place called Lynde. The priest was there and we asked permission to try the organ. Nearby was a large transport camp. As I played a few well-known hymns a few soldiers drifted in, then more and more, till there were sixty or more men there, nearly filling the little church. We had a great time, the men calling out for their favourite hymns. We all enjoyed it very much and went on till twilight came. A few months after this, on my way home for good, I stayed the night at Hazebrook, and in the YMCA I was talking to a fellow musician when a man sitting the other side of him mentioned this evening at Lynde, and was delighted when I told him I was the organist.

After I came home from the war I was organist at Glemsford for three years. Then in 1922 I went to Clare, where I played for twenty-two years. We had a fine choir there and we were a very happy company. Although I retired from regular organist's work in 1944 I have helped out at various churches for long or short periods of service and have substituted for holidays or in cases of sickness ever since.

About thirteen years ago I went to play at Cornard and in the congregation was Mr. Alfred Bull, formerly of Borley, by now aged well over ninety. We knew each other very well when I was organist at Borley, so after the service I made myself known to him. He hesitated a bit then said, "Oh yes, I do remember you," then after a pause he continued. "We had a strange organist in church this morning and we didn't get on very well!"

Music has always given me tremendous joy and happiness. It has brought me in touch with many interesting people in all walks of life, and I have had opportunities to play in many places. As an organist I have always tried to use music to enrich the worship. I've always felt music should "speak"; that it should interpret the hymns and the exquisite beauty of the psalms. As a choirmaster my aim has always been to get the choir to sing with understanding of the words they were singing.

14

Bell-Ringing

Bells and bell-ringing have been a subject of interest for thousands of years. I've read that the oldest bell in the world was found near Babylon and is reputed to be over 3,000 years old. Bells for horses are mentioned in the Bible, in Zechariah. From old records we learn that the first bell was cast in England by Abbot Turketulus and was hung in Crowland Abbey, Lincolnshire, about 1,400 years ago. The largest known bell was cast in Russia in 1733. It weighed 193 tons, but was never rung.

In Melford we have records of change-ringing for the last 250 years. "Beere for the ringers" appears in many of the old church records, and at Clare they had a special pitcher for the ringers, still preserved in a glass case. People often say to me, "It must be hard work ringing bells," but it is not physically hard, although the heavier bells do need more strength than the lighter ones. To pull a bell correctly needs precision and balance, and once you have mastered that you can go on pulling bells with ease till you are well over ninety.

When I was fifteen (in 1893) I got very interested in bell-ringing. I used to go up the tower to watch the ringers at work, and before long I learnt the correct way to pull a bell. But it was change-ringing which interested me more. This art, which originated in England, is a method of producing different changes in the note sequences, and it is a fascinating pastime. This is mentally hard work, for the patterns of change-ringing are based on mathematical permutations and combinations of great complexity and the ringer must carry them all in his memory. The secret of success is concentration, and farm workers may easily be better ringers than professional men because their monotonous work gives them time to memorise the intricate methods.

These methods of change-ringing have all sorts of odd interesting titles given to them, such as Grandsire, Double Norwich Court, Superlative Surprise. In the seventeenth century Fabian Stedman, a Cambridge printer, composed a very popular method named Stedman's principle and this is still in use. These changes can be rung on varying numbers of bells, and the table opposite, which sets out the number of possible changes on a given number of bells, may be of interest.

Melford Church has eight bells, but my first ambition was to ring 720 changes on six bells. At the same time, however, a local butcher was also very keen to do so. So keen in fact was he that he promised a leg of mutton supper to the ringers if they could help him to achieve his aim. They all tried hard to help him, giving him advice from every direction, and he too tried hard, but he never succeeded. In the meantime I just had to sit and watch, but thereby I gained a lot of knowledge of the method. As soon as an opportunity was offered to take part in a complete peal of 720 changes I seized it, and managed to get through. From then on I was accepted as a ringing member of the band.

My first peal on eight bells was on 20 November 1895, and took three hours fifteen minutes. The next peal in which I took

No of bells	Name	No of changes	Time needed			
			Years	Days	Hours	Minutes
4	Minimus	24				1
5	Doubles	120				5
6	Minor	720				30
7	Triples	5,040			3	30
8	Major	40,032		1	4	
9	Caters	362,880		10	12	
10	Royal	3,628,800		105		
11	Cinques	39,916,800	3	60		
12	Maximus	479,001,600	37	355		

part was on 2 May 1896 at St. Mary's, Bury St. Edmunds, and these being heavier bells, took three hours thirty-five minutes. There is a peal board in the church tower recording this event and I am the only survivor of this peal.

There are two interesting peal boards in Melford tower with quaint wording. One is dated 26 September 1768.

Within this steeple was rung complete
A peal of Treble Bob, with music sweet;
By the Melford company as doth appear!
And if their names you'd know, why here they are:
James Ward as first the Treble he did ring,
Samuel Scott the second he did nicely swing;
Young Cutts, the Miller, with the third did play,
Jeremiah Heard the fourth did sway;

The fifth was rung by John Pearson,
William Smith the sixth being next in turn;
John Corder the seventh, and the peal did call,
George Cadge, the tenor, which completed them all;
Within three hours and ten minutes space,
It was all over, and each bell had run its race.
The changes were five thousand and six score,
Them being done there was no need for more.

From the extravagant wording of the following verse the ringers were evidently highly delighted with their achievement on 22 July 1782.

Attend ye Gods, Oh! hark ye Saints Divine,
Give merit to a ringer's rhyme;
No trifling peal, I mean, no paltry change,
London Court Bob, that peal of mighty range;
And here as in the following time are named,
These were the men for ringing highly famed;
Samuel Scott as first, with the Treble he did lead,
The second was rung by Joshua Steed;
Joseph Cutts, the third, stood well in place,
John Pearson, the fourth bell swayed in the chase;
James Green, the fifth of whom stood much in need,
And the sixth was rung by William Smith indeed;
John Corder, the seventh, and the peal did call,
George Cadge, the Tenor, which completed them all.
The changes were five thousand and twice one score,
And it is supposed 'twas never done before.
Within three hours and ten minutes space,
And the changes took no ringer from his place.

There used to be some bell founders in Sudbury. Henry Pleasants, who was noted for the punning rhymes he put on his bells, had a foundry near an old timber yard in King Street between 1694 and 1707. Later it was moved to Hospital Yard near Ballingdon Bridge and later still to Curds Lane and carried on by John Thornton (1708 to 1720) and Thomas Gardiner (1709 to 1759).

I was always very interested and often amused at the peculiarities of ringers when in action. Some would stand with their eyes shut so tight one could imagine they were asleep, but no doubt they were concentrating deeply on the method. Some would make the most extraordinary grimaces in the intensity of their concentration. Some would make heavy going of it, and others would appear to take it casually and lightly.

One learner had such an awkward way of handling the bell rope (and there is danger in this if it is not done correctly) that his instructor said, "Be careful of that rope. If you hang me you'll have to keep my missus." One old boy I remember used to twirl his arm over his head at regular intervals. There was an old ringer at Glemsford who had two round feet, like stumps, but he could climb the steeples with the rest of us. He had his hair done in ringlets, most quaint and old-fashioned.

One old Sudbury ringer was trying for a long peal when his vigorous pulling made his belt slip and become separated from the top of his trousers. But he was far too interested in his ringing to be deterred by that, and he called out to the conductor, "My trousers are coming down but don't stop." He stood for the rest of the peal with his trousers over his boots and his long shirt hanging round his legs like a kilt. In spite of the amusing incident the ringers were not put off and completed their peal.

When I first started ringing there were many good bands in the neighbourhood and some of us would join them from time to time. I remember one very enjoyable occasion when I went to Lavenham with an old ringer, Bentlin Ambrose (no relation). To me he seemed a very old man (he was about sixty). He had a little beard and lots of whiskers, out of which constantly stuck a little clay pipe. He was a very good ringer, and pulled his rope straight down in front of his nose with a steady even stroke. He was a man of few words but enjoyed a joke, even against himself. His friends often teased him because on his wedding night a fire broke out in the village, and hearing shouting and noise he jumped out of bed and went to watch the fire.

It was a very hot summer's day when we went on our little expedition. We stopped at the Hare for a pint to fortify ourselves before walking across the fields to Lavenham. We went down Hare Drift, past the gamekeeper's cottage, along some fields near a farm and across the stream at Spratford. We paused, as we always did, when we crossed the two planks over the stream, as there were some very fine pike here. Then on over the railway line to Lavenham. We went straight up the tower and joined the other ringers where we stood for three hours twenty minutes and succeeded in getting the peal. We then adjourned to the Cock for a bread-and-cheese tea. Here we met some dealers and other old friends and spent a thoroughly enjoyable evening in their company. At eleven o'clock we walked home via Bridge Street, to the accompaniment of the hooting of the owls and other nocturnal animal sounds. It was a grand way of spending a Saturday afternoon and evening.

The Lavenham bells are specially lovely and have a rich tone. Some ringers think they are the finest in England. The tenor bell, which is said by some to have "the sweetest voice" in England, was cast by Miles Graye of Colchester in 1625. Its birthday is celebrated every year in June, as near as possible to the 21st, when bells are rung all day long in its honour. I remember standing on the Green at Melford one New Year's Eve at midnight and listening to the Lavenham bells. It was a clear bright night and the music of the bells came floating gently across the quiet countryside. It was almost a heavenly experience, such beauty and peace, an unforgettable memory.

One Boxing Day Fred Connell, two others and I drove over to Lavenham in a dog cart to try for a long peal. There was nearly a foot of snow and when we arrived at Lavenham we had some long time to await the arrival of a man from Preston to make up our team. So what else could we do but adjourn to the Cock Inn. Here we indulged in several potions of hot rum which went down very nicely on such a cold day. In due course the Preston man arrived and we went up the tower. After a short while someone made a mistake, so we started again. Then a second ringer lost his place, and we made a second attempt. But we'd not got far when I went wrong, whereupon the conductor said, "Ernie, you ought to know better. It's time we packed up." I'm afraid rum was the real cause of our breakdown.

Sometimes one or two of us would walk down to Sudbury on Saturday evenings and join the ringers in their practice. We'd have a ring at St. Peter's and perhaps adjourn to the Black Boy for a wet before going on to All Saints to have a pull there. Usually after that we'd go into the nearby hostelry, the Bull, where we'd enjoy a sausage supper for about sixpence and be entertained by the assembled company. I can still see them now sitting round the smoke room. There was always a group of old stagers at this pub, some of the old bargees, with long beards and thick whiskers, one or two of them with gold ear-rings. They'd sit and smoke their long churchwarden pipes which were kept for them in a stand on the table. They'd have their own special beer mugs. They were rare characters and very good company. After a very pleasant evening with them and a good meal we were ready for our walk back to Melford.

We came down one Saturday evening for a practice and found the church door at St. Peter's locked. We could hear the organ playing inside so we went to find the verger. He was a fierce-looking sort of fellow and, as usual, he had had three or four. He got hold of a broom and charged at the church door – bang, bang, bang. The Market Hill being quiet, and almost no traffic about, the noise resounded. Some wag called out, "Come in," which didn't improve the verger's temper. "I'll show you who's verger here," he shouted. Whereupon a meek-looking young man gently opened the church door, shaking like a leaf. He explained he was only practising on the organ and had locked the door to keep people out.

We always enjoyed ringing the bells at St. Peter's, but the tradespeople didn't think much of it as the sound was so much on top of them, and as the shops kept open late in those days they couldn't hear themselves or their customers speak, so we were not very popular.

Some of the old ringers told me that when Prince Bertie married Princess Alexandra on 10 March 1863, the Sudbury ringers decided they'd like to ring during the wedding ceremony. As the marriage was to take place during Lent the rector refused the ringers permission and to enforce his prohibition he took the key of the ringing chamber home with him. But his opposition made the ringers all the more determined and they made plans to get round the problem. On their last practice night before the wedding they left the door of the belfry, which opened onto the roof, unlocked. When the wedding day arrived they got to the church early and with the aid of a ladder they climbed the first part of the church, then drawing it up after them, succeeded in reaching the belfry. It was a risky operation. They waited till the time of the wedding and then the bells rang out merrily. The townspeople (who had heard rumours of the controversy) were highly delighted, but the rector was furious.

On the occasion of Queen Victoria's diamond jubilee in March 1897, the Melford company rang a complete peal of 5,040 changes of the method called Plain Bob Triples. As far as we could trace this was the first peal in that method by a Melford band. It took three hours ten minutes and was conducted by Charles Bixby. Those taking part were Tom Cadge, Henry Duce, Fred Connell, Amor Ambrose, Sam Ford, Harry Richold, and myself. It was composed by H. Hubbard.

The Rev. G.St.J. Topham (rector from 1892 to 1902) was always very helpful to the ringers and we got on well together. We used regularly to climb the church tower on the last day of the old year and ring in the new (one enthusiastic ringer said he had rung the new year in hundreds of times!), and the Rev. Topham would always invite us into the rectory afterwards where he'd have a bowl of hot punch waiting to share with us. We used to discuss ringing and I remember the New Year of 1897 when he talked about the old brick tower and said, "I am not a rich man, but I am willing to contribute £1,000 towards a new tower." He followed up this promise by calling together a meeting of the parishioners and this ultimately resulted in the building of the new church tower as it is today.

We ringers used to hold an annual supper and on one

occasion we invited the Rev. Topham as our guest. The supper was held at the Scutchers Arms and the landlord, Charlie Bixby, roasted a large leg of mutton on a spit over a roaring fire; while it revolved round and round the dripping fat fell on to a huge delicious pudding. The rector said it was the best meal he'd had in his life.

One Sunday after we had rung for early service Peter (Stewart) Richold, who was of an inventive turn of mind, persuaded us to go down to his house in Westgate Street to have our photos taken. As there was snow on the ground he decided the light was good for his experiment. He had made a camera out of a wooden box in which he'd fixed a lens and shutter. He fixed the camera on a post, then at intervals he placed four more posts on which he'd put pulley wheels. He then fastened a string on the shutter of the camera and brought it along the posts through the wheels.

He placed us all in position then came and stood beside us. He shouted to us all to pay attention, then pulled the string. Up went the shutter – but alas it refused to fall. He was so annoyed he gave the string a fierce jerk and the whole contraption collapsed amidst roars of laughter from the ringers. But Peter didn't see the joke. Anyway it was too cold to stand out in his yard, so we all adjourned to Brusley (Henry) Duce's house on the Green, where he regaled us with home-made wine, still laughing at the incident. But Peter wasn't beaten. He tried several more times and finally succeeded in taking quite a good photo of us all. You can see the posts in the photo and Peter standing alongside us; only the initiated would know about the string.

We used to learn change-ringing methods on handbells. On special occasions we would take these handbells out to different functions to give entertainment. At Christmas time especially we would visit farms and some of the big houses and give them some ringing on the bells. We were always very welcome. We'd start off with good resolutions, determined to keep sober long enough to visit about six places. But when we got to the friendly houses we'd be invited inside and in their cosy kitchens be treated so generously it was hard to leave.

After about three or four such jolly and delightful visits we couldn't get further and had to make our way home. Getting over stiles was a rare job, but great fun. The more lively ones would try to balance on the top bar – then splosh! Then we'd discover one of our party was missing and we'd all go back over the stile to look for him. It was not too bad on a moonlit night but on dark nights we had to carry lanterns as well as our bells, and we kept losing one or other. But we always took great care of our bells.

Bell-ringing opens up many opportunities to meet people and ringers are welcome in any town or village where bells are rung. When away from home I've usually tried to go to the local church in case I should happen on a few ringers. Here you can meet men and women, and youngsters too, all keenly interested in campanology. I've enjoyed some lovely times amongst the ringing fraternity and have joined ringers as far afield as St. Clements Danes Church, London, St. Marys, Warwick, the Isle of Wight and Devon, and of course in a large number of local churches, and have always found a welcome.

15

MELFORD BAND

Mr. George Whittle started a Drum and Fife Band in 1890 and quite a few of the mat-makers joined, but although they tried hard to make a go of it, it only lasted for two or three years. I still have one of the fifes they used.

In 1894 the Melford Brass Band was formed and Mr. Glazin, who was much admired, became their first bandmaster. They were an enthusiastic company of men and would march up and down the village blowing full-blast on their instruments, making many weird noises. They had music in front of them, but I doubt whether many of them could read it. The cornet player could, and he played the air fortissimo, while most of the others went boom...boom...boom on the same note. They attended functions and got high praise from the local newspapers. They were good fellows and they certainly persevered. After a while, however, a military bandsman from Sudbury named Foster took over, and he taught them to read music and to play scales. From this point on one could hear scales being practised with great gusto on all sorts of instruments in cottages up and down the village. How the neighbours must have blessed them!

A number of the bandsmen who were also members of the Old Volunteer Corps of the 5th Suffolk Regiment gave their services as bandsmen to the Company, and this added considerably to their prestige.

The band continued to be in great demand for local fêtes and functions in the neighbourhood. It has since become the Melford Silver Band, has gained a reputation for high-class performances, and has won many awards in competitions over the years against very good bands in the country.

16

Inns and Public Houses and their Customers

The church and the public houses were the chief meeting places of the people when I was a boy. Here they would gather and exchange news and views, and from both these centres the life of the village emanated. I am not sure which of the two exerted the most powerful influence on people's lives.

I must say though that many of the pubs were very attractive. They were cosy and warm and one could always find a kindred spirit ready to talk and to have a laugh with, whatever time of day. A good laugh is a great tonic, a relaxation from tension and worries. Many people went to the pubs just for company and to meet friends, not necessarily to drink a great deal. I went chiefly for this reason. I've always enjoyed meeting people and hearing about their interests, and peculiarities too; and the pubs, especially the old-fashioned friendly ones, were the places to find them.

I can still picture quite easily the rare characters I knew in those days; they were really great men, and I laugh to myself as I recall the fun and jolly times we had together. I've always been an interested spectator of the great game of life which we all play in our own small way. We had time in those days to get to know one another, and time to enjoy one another's company. Many of the cottages were overcrowded and had little comfort, and the men would escape from their family problems by coming to the warm little pubs which provided them with a comfortable bolt-hole, while very often the womenfolk would be glad to "git riddy on 'em" for a while. Unfortunately some of the men spent more time in the pubs than at work; then the wives would rear up and the band played!

Many ladies of the village were quite capable of dealing with their husbands if things got too bad. Some would come and haul their man out of the pub and run him home. "I'll sole 'is skull fa 'im." Woe unto the man who fell down on his doorstep, as the lady of the house would take it out of him if he couldn't get up. I've known more than one man who, if he fell down, daren't call to his wife for help. His pals would ask him afterwards, "Why didn't you call the missus?" "Ah, that's jes' what she'd a-liked. She'd a-played 'ell with me." But with beer so cheap and plentiful and the gravity so high it was no wonder there was so much drunkenness. It was commonplace to see a man, or even a woman, rolling about the street, quite incapable. Beer was so cheap they'd even give it to their animals. My father mixed old beer with the bran and swill he gave his pigs and they thrived on it. It smelt so good I could have eaten it myself. I remember an old chap with a donkey cart who came through Melford regularly to Sudbury market. He'd stop at the Lion for a drink and his old donkey obstinately refused to move till he'd had his pint of stout.

Melford had a generous share of such hostelries and could boast of thirteen along her main street within a distance of not much more than two miles. There was the Perseverance, the

White Hart, White Horse, Cross Keys (now a private house), King William (now Gardiner's Garage), George and Dragon, Swan, Bull, Cock and Bell, Crown, Black Lion, Scutchers Arms, the Hare, and just before my time there used to be the Ram between the chemist and Coconut House.

Hall Street, George and Dragon, c. 1900-5.
From print owned by A. Cadge, Esq.

The pubs used to brew their own beer at that time, or employ someone to come in and do it for them. It was a very important trade and had to be done carefully and accurately. They had several grades and the lowest grade could be sold for as little as a penny a pint. Many of the villagers, too, brewed their own beer. We had a large barrel in the corner of one of our front rooms, which held about thirty gallons, and father brewed a consignment as required. Some people made what they called sharp beer, like vinegar. One mat-maker wouldn't have any other.

The hospital men used to brew every October. They had some very large barrels in their cellars. I believe they held 100 gallons each. They'd keep some at least of this beer for a whole year before using it. It was beautiful stuff, better than any wine. One day when I was about seven years old I was sent up there with a message for Mr. Spilling, the warden. He was a nice old gentleman and very civil. He said, "Would you like a taste of old beer, boy?" "Yes please sir." It tasted very nice indeed, but when I got outside I seemed to be climbing up hill to go down the Green, and I had a job to find my own house. When I got inside my little stool seemed to be floating round. I didn't know what was the matter with me, but Ma did, and she took me firmly by the shoulders and marched me off to bed.

Most of the inns had a tap room and a smoke room or bar parlour. The tap room was where the lesser lights gathered – those who preferred the cheaper prices for the lower grades of beer – while the smoke room was patronised by tradesmen and more prosperous gentlemen. Floors, often earth, were sprinkled with sand or sawdust. Round iron spittoons were provided and used (not always very accurately) and cleaned and emptied according to the whim and inclination of the landlord. If windows were made to open it was not always very apparent and in consequence the atmosphere got thick and heavy with a prevailing smell of stale beer and tobacco. They often boasted a big glass case containing a huge pike or stuffed otter caught locally or some brightly plumed birds, and more often than not a flyblown picture of Queen Victoria.

People travelling through the village would stop and have a rest and a wet. Travelling artists came and stopped long enough to do some painting or drawing on the walls of these old inns, probably in payment for their refreshment or a night's lodging.

At the Black Lion there are greyhounds drawn on the wall, and at the Hare there are two very fine paintings of country scenes above the chimney from the mantelpiece to the ceiling.

From my own long and not inconsiderable experience, all the Melford pubs were run by friendly, jovial landlords. It's no wonder at all that men spent so much time in these warm and homely inns. In the Bull hotel there was a stand in which the regular customers put their churchwarden pipes, a clay with a very long stem. Each man knew his own pipe and left it there ready to enjoy on his next visit. Sometimes a customer would have his own mug reserved for him too, and even a special seat. I can still see in my mind the comfortable smoke room at the Cock and Bell and Tup Cadge sitting in his favourite corner seat. On the shelf above him was a glass with a large bowl for his whisky. Tup was a big, rotund heavy-built man, always jovial and ready for a laugh. He was a boot-maker and had a shop in Hall Street.

The landlords would vie with one another as to who could put on the best dinner for the cheapest price. I remember the landlord of the Glemsford Lion, a man called Game. He used to serve a splendid meal. He was a fine upstanding man and used to drive through Melford on his way to Sudbury market in a smart dog cart, cracking his whip and calling out to friends. Some of the Melford wags would crack up his good dinners and he'd fall for their flattery. They probably got extra helpings, the artful devils. Talking of good dinners though, it was hard to beat Mrs. Hales, who ran a little shop opposite the mat factory a few doors from the Bull. For sixpence she gave you roast chicken, Yorkshire pudding and two vegetables – and large helpings at that.

One of the most noted and popular landlords I ever knew

was Billy Bareham at Clare Bell. I often went there for a drink after playing for service at the church. Billy was well-known over a wide area and his meals were excellent, his wife being a very good cook. His charming manner endeared him to everyone who called at his pub.

I remember too the landlord at Alpheton Lion, Sam Clements; he was a real old-fashioned jovial fellow. He was a crack shot and would train people to shoot while riding horseback. He had a habit of inviting his patrons to dinner. "Come on in, old boy, and stay to dinner." They thought this was a free do, but got sucked in. After a tip-top dinner of generous proportions he'd say, "That'll be two and six please." Not many were caught twice.

The Fir Trees at Cavendish (now alas no more) was another popular place to call. King Richardson was the landlord here, a great friend of my father's. He was a bluff, hearty man, a real John Bull type. I often called on my way home from Clare and we'd have a drink together in the evening. I used to say, "Have a last one with me, King." "No, bor, I 'ont 'ave no more." (Then in an undertone) "I want to be so as I ken spake to she civil in the mornin'."

The Hare was a popular place with us and we very much liked the landlord, Peter Richold. He was genial and friendly and knew how to handle people. Later on Mr. Drage came to the Hare and he too was a great favourite, a rare character in a quiet way. Large numbers of travellers on the road called at the Hare, as it was the last pub in Melford. It was quite a long way to the Alpheton Lion and it was dry work driving a horse and cart along a dusty road.

I can still picture the patrons of the Hare. There were always a few gamekeepers sitting there together "well-britched" in their fustian cloth suits. These were made to measure by a tailor from Mildenhall who came over once a year and stayed at the Hare. The keepers were supplied with one suit a year, paid for by their employers. Their discarded suits were much in demand as they were such hard-wearing garments. Brown buskins were worn with them – quite a smart outfit. As well as a lot of farm labourers who lived in the High Street area, we also had a number of tradesmen who usually sat together, looking prosperous in their bowler hats with their heavy turnip watches suspended across their well-filled waistcoats.

The older generation of Suffolk men were cautious and suspicious in their dealings with one another and even more so with strangers. They spoke in a roundabout way and avoided direct questions and answers. It was in their nature to be evasive and indirect and they were always very guarded. I've often noticed this trait and wondered whether it stemmed from their long history of living in a part of the country so often subjected to foreign invasions. "Arter 'e sed what 'e did I gie 'im a sole o' the skull." If you asked, "Well what did he say?" You'd probably get the reply, "Ah 'e knowed what 'e say." It didn't incriminate the speaker.

Another characteristic I have noticed, especially when I have gone into a pub where I was not known. The customers would cautiously eye me up and down and conversation would cease. If they approved of me, talk would very gradually start flowing again. But you had to feel your way before you could join in and be accepted. Once you get to know Suffolk people, they are very friendly, but occasionally someone would be cold-shouldered and the reason given would be, "Ah, 'e 'ant knock in with the likes o' we."

Suffolk men of this period enjoyed pretending they were

ignorant oafs when it suited their purpose. I think this amusing pastime is still practised among some of the older folk. They specially enjoyed this pretence when a "furriner" came into the pub, more especially if he was an official of any sort, or a man of some authority. They were always fair game for their sport. It was fatal for anyone who was not familiar with the crowd to put on airs and graces or to boast of his achievements. He had his leg pulled unmercifully. Occasionally a visitor from London would appear, dressed in smart city clothes, and if he put on an air of patronising condescension he was sure to be subjected to this treatment. They would do it with such an air of innocence that the stranger more often than not would be quite unaware that they were getting at him, and really thought they were a lot of stupid ignorant countrymen. They would ask such simple naive questions and listen so attentively to his replies, hanging on to his words as though he were an oracle. If he was particularly boastful about his achievements they would press him further, and appear to be deeply impressed, while the onlookers would murmur from time to time "Ar, Ar". When his back was turned they would roar with laughter.

They enjoyed baiting each other in a similar way, asking oblique questions and more often than not getting an oblique answer in reply. This sort of quick-witted nonsense and clever repartee created good entertainment and we all enjoyed ourselves. In the smoke room at the Hare one night a visitor to the village, a Mr. Drage from Leeds, was so elated by the leg-pulling that he stood drinks round the room twice, saying it was better than any music hall entertainment he'd ever seen.

One evening at the Hare gardening was the subject under discussion. Many of the men had allotments and they would look over each other's bit of land and criticise without mercy.

A retired policeman from London, named Debbidge, used the Hare a lot, and this evening he was being entertained with exaggerated tales about the enormous size of local grown potatoes. He seemed so taken in by it that Bill Fakes, the gamekeeper who lived up Hare Drift, said to him, "Would you like to see a nice root of they big taters, bor? Come along tomorrow mornin' and I'll show you some." Next morning when he saw Debbidge coming up the lane, he got his gun, starting off out, pretending he'd forgotten the visit. As Debbidge approached he said, "Ah, I'd forgotten about you. But there, the missus wants some taters fer dinner, you can help me dig some." (He had previously buried a quantity of extra large potatoes round a root.) He dug carefully, filling up a pail with these big ones, then said, "There, you pull the root." The incredulous policeman was amazed: "Never in my life have I seen such a fine lot."

For a few days nothing was said about the incident, but a few of Fakes' friends were told about it and gradually remarks were heard in the Hare such as "Ah, you orter see what I see. A whole pail of taters orf one root." Further pauses, then up came the subject again. "No I never seed such taters afore. Sich a size." Debbidge was listening. "Did you see 'em orl come orf one root?" Then suddenly his jaw fell and he began to see daylight. Of course the fun and laughter and repetition of the joke lasted a long time.

One warm summer's night there were an extra large number of frogs on Clappits pond and their croaking made a master noise. Some wag told Debbidge the noise came from Cockney crows. Some of the locals heard about this and when the retired policeman came into the Hare again they remarked about the strange noises coming from the pond:

"Oh, they're Cockney crows," said Debbidge.

"Goo on, are they? Well, I never heerd tell o' that afore. Who telled ya?"

"Jack ......" (a notorious legpuller).

"Well it must be right then!"

Cockney crows cropped up in conversations for a long time after that.

They lived on humour in those days. It was their whole way of life. They had very little respect for one another or their achievements and they took all the baiting in good part and were always ready to tell a joke against themselves. It was all part of their light-hearted attitude to life. Shonk Pleasants came into the Hare one day and announced:

"There's a play coming to Sudbury next week called *The Forty Thieves* and they say they are short of two thieves."

"Tell 'em ta come down 'ere then," said Bogey, "we can let 'em have a couple!"

Alec Hurst ran a little cycle shop in Hall Street and he loved to boast about his "business". Some pals of his saw a notice on his door one day "Out on business. Back in three minutes." They added to that note "Try the Bull, Crown or Cock and Bell."

A regular frequenter of the Hare smoke room was an old soldier, a knowly sort of chap who made himself rather a nuisance because of his insistent boasting. He was a cavalryman, very good with horses, who served in the Boer war and reckoned he knew everyone else who did so. One of the gamekeepers got so fed up with this that he proclaimed to a friend sitting nearby (loud enough for the old soldier to hear), "We're getting a new under-keeper soon, a young chap, and I hear he was in the Boer war." The old soldier immediately pricked up his ears and asked the name.

Gamekeeper: "Barnes."
Old soldier: "What regiment was he in?"
Keeper: (Had to think a bit) "The Artillery."
Soldier: "What battery?"
Keeper: (This was a poser, but he ventured a shot.) "L.
Battery." (There was no such battery).
Soldier: "Oh that was old Charlie Barnes. I knew him
quite well."
Keeper: "I'll introduce you to him when he comes."

In due course the young man appeared and it was obvious he was far too young ever to have been to South Africa, but he had been well-primed by the keeper and he played the part. They were duly introduced and interested onlookers watched the charade with great amusement. The gamekeeper, a serious-looking chap with a round red face, kept up the pretence and the old soldier bought drinks for the two of them, and he was so excited about it all that he never stopped to think the new man was far too young to have served in the war. You can imagine how the assembled company enjoyed the joke, and the hoax continued indefinitely as far as I can remember.

I remember Bill Hinchcliff, a Yorkshire man, who was a skilled dyer at Lists Horsehair Factory. In the Hare one day he said, "I've never heard a nightingale down this way. We have a lot where I come from up North." We couldn't let that remark pass, and someone said, "Phew, yes, we have a master lot of nightingales round here. We'll show you some." We had a gamekeeper, Joe Mortlock, who was a clever mimic of bird song. So they arranged for Joe to be in Kentwell Avenue one night, and then got Bill to go along with them to hear the nightingales sing. At a given signal the "nightingale" began to sing. "Phew. That's wonderful. Didn't know you had such lovely ones." He was very impressed. I wondered whether he had really been deceived or not, so a few days later I brought up the subject of birds. Then he told me about the lovely nightingales he had heard in Kentwell Avenue. I don't think he was ever disillusioned.

Dealers would come into the pubs and were fond of boasting about their wealth, especially on market days. They'd put their long leather bags on the table, show off their golden sovereigns and boast, "I can buy the lot of you. All on ya." One day a workman, who probably hadn't much more than fourpence, said he could produce ten gold sovereigns, but someone called out, "You ... You couldn't produce ten bob let along ten sovereigns." The argument continued and bets were made, which was just what the man wanted. "Orl right I'll goo 'ome and git 'em." Instead he went round the back door of the pub and borrowed ten sovereigns from the landlord. To the astonishment of all the company he produced them and won his bet.

The landlords were easygoing fellows and never minded if someone called at the tap room door selling fish to their customers. In fact I think they were quite pleased as it made them all the more thirsty. Bloaters were popular and could be bought at a penny a time, or perhaps a penny-halfpenny for an extra big one. They would fry them themselves on a grid or shovel over the tap-room fire, which would flare up and sizzle as the fat dropped into the flames and the fish got blacker. "Give us a pennoth o' bread governor," they'd call out to the landlord and they'd eat it up, bones and all. For some this would be their only meal of the day.

One day at the Hare our old groom from the mat factory, Frank Snell, got into an argument with another fellow who was frying on the same shovel, as to whose fish was the biggest. The row developed so fiercely they went outside to fight it out, and the result was that Frank got a broken nose. I never heard what happened to the bloater.

I remember an occasion when my father and two friends hired a pony and trap from the Cock and Bell to go to Bury to see a performance by Buffalo Bill. Freddy Neal, the proprietor, drove them. They must have had a wonderful day at the show and met many jovial friends who shared their jollifications at various hostelries in the town. On their way home, however, they couldn't possibly pass the Bradfield Manger, so turned in just to have a last one. But it was midnight closing time before they finally left and by now they all had to be helped or pushed into the trap. The driver could just manage to give the pony a gee-up before sinking to sleep over the reins. A mile or two along the road the trap must have given a lurch over an extra big stone or rut, and one of the revellers fell out of the back; but he was not missed and the pony continued to jog along patiently. Somewhere near Alpheton the second rear passenger fell out, unknown to the pair in front. When they reached Kentwell Hall gates my father was just about capable of stopping the pony and climbing out, and he staggered home. The old pony went on down Melford street and finally came to a halt at the Cock and Bell. The lady of the house heard the clop, clop of the pony's hoofs, then silence. She climbed out of bed and looked out of the window and there was her husband sound asleep, slumped across the front of the trap, the reins dangling from his hands. Some reports say she let him stay there till morning.

But there, it was not an unusual occurrence.

I remember a light-fingered gentleman who was always a nuisance to the police. He was in the Maldon Grey at Sudbury one day when the landlord asked him if he had any work. When he said no, the landlord said, "Will you come up early tomorrow and brush my walnut trees? The boys are such a nuisance." And he agreed to do it. He was well up the tree, busy on the job, when a policeman came along. "Ah, I've got you this time. Come on down." Down he came and immediately started running down the road and round the meadows with the policeman running after him. Finally, back he came to the walnut tree. The landlord, hearing a commotion, looked out of his window and asked what was amiss. "Nawthen pertic'lar only 'e want ta take me in fer a-brushing ya walnut tree." The landlord explained the situation and the policeman retired discomfited.

This same gentleman was at work at Acton shortly after, on a farm. One day the farmer asked him if he'd take a bag of brussels sprouts to the police inspector at Sudbury. About a mile from the town he was accosted by a policeman who asked what he'd got in the bag.

"Wass that ta do with ya?"

"Nawthen; but ya'd better come along a me."

"Are ya a-goin' ta tak me ta the station?"

"Yes I am."

"Then you'll ha ta carry the sack. I on't."

The policeman duly took up the bag and carried it all the way to Sudbury police station. When the inspector saw them come in he said, "What is it this time?" "Nawthen much," said the culprit. "Mr. Stennett asked me ta bring these 'ere sprouts what you ordered. The policeman sed I was ta come along a 'im. And 'e kindly carried the bag fer me. Wasn't that civil on 'im ?" The policeman enjoyed the joke and was fond of telling this tale against himself.

We used to have some very enjoyable horkeys at the Hare. A lot of farm hands lived up High Street and so the Hare was a favourite place to hold these annual celebrations. Several women would bake huge Yorkshire puddings with a large joint in the middle and bring them along to the pub. They were delicious. We celebrated with enthusiasm and abandonment and thoroughly enjoyed ourselves, singing all the old-fashioned folk songs popular at that time.

Christmas too was a grand time for celebrations and the pubs provided a good meeting place. Hot beer and gin was a popular drink then, especially if the winter was a bit cold. Someone would call out, "Give us half a pint and a pennoth and hot it up." This was half a pint of the best beer for a penny and a tot of gin for another penny. The landlord would pour this into a funnel-like container which he stuck into the fire to warm up. It was lovely and made you glow all over.

As it came up towards Christmas many of the pubs organised a raffle and the prizes, needless to say, were bottles of drink. Gin was one shilling and ninepence a bottle, whisky about two shillings and sixpence to three shillings, and brandy three shillings and sixpence to four shillings. We'd all save up about sixpence or so and for this we'd get quite a few tickets. From my recollections of these early Christmas Eves most of us left the pubs, when they did finally close, with bottles of some sort sticking out of our pockets, whether we got them by raffle tickets or some other way. We'd all help each other home, singing lustily to assist us on the way.

I can remember one specially memorable occasion when my

father and his friend saw each other home three times, on each occasion going into their houses and having another little tot for friendship's sake. On what they decided would be their final farewell, the friend discovered he'd lost a parcel somewhere near the pound trees. He'd been carrying this around with him all evening. It was six pounds of beef given to him by his boss for a Christmas present. So of course back they had to go to search for the parcel. I don't remember what the time was when they finally arrived at their respective homes.

It was not at all unusual after a jolly evening at the local for gentlemen to find themselves in the wrong house. They'd slump down in the front room in the nearest available space and go fast asleep. If the owner of the house heard them he or she would come down and turf them out, but it has been known for some to sleep all night in the wrong house and not be found till morning. I once had a jolly evening out and found myself in the wrong house. When I felt the wall it was on the wrong side! I cautiously slid out and equally cautiously crept into my own house next door, taking care not to wake the household. Mind you, in those days there were no street lights at all and it was very easy to go into the wrong door on a dark night.

We did crazy things at turning-out times, especially if some of us had got a bit merry – things like climbing the nearest tree, seeing who could get the highest, and singing and shouting. But if the policeman was spotted we'd scramble down quick and soon scarper off home. We'd play tricks like pulling down the barber's pole and planting it in the river, or tying a cartwheel to a tree or gate, or some such prank, which may perhaps sound schoolboyish, but they were just high spirits and never vicious or cruel.

Skittles and quoits were popular games and several of the

pubs provided facilities for these pastimes. The Black Lion had a skittles alley in that long shed at the side. The skittles or nine pins were big and heavy, and the "cheese" which was thrown at them was large and heavy too, nearly a foot in diameter. It was a very noisy game on the wooden floor, but great fun. One chap would set up the skittles and one was appointed to pour out the beer. There was never a lack of volunteers for this important job. He'd collect a gallon or more of beer and some of the coarse brown earthenware mugs, much approved of by the customers (it "drinked better" out of them) and preferred to the pewter ones used in some of the pubs, and keep them replenished during the evening. He'd set his wares up alongside the skittle alley and was kept very busy.

The Hare had an outdoor bed for quoits. It was made of clay and had a thick iron peg stuck in the middle. If rings were not available horseshoes would be used. This was a very enjoyable game and teams played against one another in the village. I remember an old chap who was on the road, who used to call at the Hare from time to time and challenge the players to a game. He had extra large and heavy iron quoits and he would guarantee to put up three out of every four ringers. His quoits were too big and heavy for the average player to throw. He'd give a performance and then take a collection, and get enough money I expect for a meal and perhaps a bed for the night. Then he would go on his travels round the country; but those quoits of his must have been very heavy to carry.

17

THE COMING OF CYCLES AND CARS

In 1891 a passenger train travelling between Lavenham and Melford at a speed of thirty-five miles an hour suddenly came off the lines as it passed Hare Drift. It plunged down the embankment dragging its five carriages with it. The engine turned completely over and the carriages tipped on their sides. Miraculously no one was killed or seriously injured.

This event naturally caused tremendous excitement and the inhabitants left what they were doing to walk or run down the Drift to see the calamity. My mother came out of her house to discuss the exciting news with her neighbours. In the meantime my small sister Connie, aged a year and a half and left to her own devices, caused a diversion by drinking some ammonia. It was dreadful to see her. She couldn't get her breath and nearly died. How my mother managed to save her life I never knew. She was a master woman in an emergency.

It was soon after this, when I was about twelve years old, that the first velocipede appeared on the streets of Melford and created great interest. It was the penny farthing or high bike, as it was called. The first designs were big heavy contraptions made by local blacksmiths with solid tyres about an inch thick. Some schemers made penny farthings with wooden spokes and rims, with iron tyres fixed to the wheel. These clumsy affairs were called bone-shakers – a most appropriate name. Men used to make them themselves. Peter (Stewart) Richold built one; he was a great schemer and could turn his hand to anything. The saddles were just behind the handle, on top of the frame, and the footrests were high up on the front fork. Common practice was to throw one foot over the front wheel to act as a brake. More daring riders would throw both legs over the handle when going down hill. I can see them now in my mind, practising up and down the casey. Some would manage to get through the rails at the bottom and some would come a cropper.

I never did try one of these bikes. They looked too much like suicide to me. But several of my friends did. They were very difficult to steer and caused many accidents and broken bones. Nevertheless people were not deterred. Two of my friends, Fred Achurch and Alec Hurst, were having a fine ride round the district and were sailing down Black Adders Hill at Acton when one of them lost control. At the bottom there is a farm gate and a sharp turn left. One succeeded in negotiating it but the other couldn't and went straight over the top. It was a few minutes before the successful rider missed his friend, but when he did he retraced his steps, calling out to him. Finally he heard a weak voice coming from a ditch. "Here I am. Couldn't stop the darned thing." He crawled out, much shaken by the experience. But in spite of all this they used to organise sports meetings on these ungainly machines, riding round grassy courses, sinking into mud and thoroughly enjoying themselves.

A few of the more adventurous ones even rode to London. Bob Sewell, Tom Ardley and Walter Hammond were the experts. It took them between five and six hours and they stayed the night and rode back next day. When you remember the bad conditions of the roads this was a real feat of endurance. Councils would spread stones and flints and farm wagons were expected to press them in while the sides were left rutted and uneven. This made roads very dangerous and when passing a horse and trap the cyclists usually jumped off. It was all right as long as the small wheel at the back didn't hit a stone, as that would make the machine tip up and overbalance.

When the first safety bicycle was seen in the parish this caused quite a sensation. It was a well-made machine with wheels of equal size – a great improvement. But it still had solid tyres. Later came the single-tube tyres with no inner tube. This was very awkward if you got a puncture, a common occurrence on our roads. Later on came the inner-tube type we have today.

A far bigger sensation was the occasion when a woman was seen on a bike. She actually cycled right through Melford street. Everyone stopped and stared, and some even ran into the road to get a better view. The women of the village were horrified, "Look at that brazen huzzy! Disgusting bit of a mawther!" She actually had baggy trousers on, tied below the knee, and black boots and stockings, and hat tied firmly on her head. She was of course riding a bike built for a man, so had to get on the back step and jump forward, or else throw her leg over like a man. However, before long bicycles were made specially for women, who took up the sport with enthusiasm.

When I grew older and was able to save up enough money I bought myself one of these bicycles specially made for me by Fred Sewell. It only cost £2 and was the best I ever had. I had many exciting adventures on it. With a friend I cycled to Clacton one weekend, through miles of fields and country lanes. There were just a few old-fashioned houses and fishermen's cottages dotted about the sea front at Clacton. We thought we had done something very impressive by cycling so far, and I still remember how exhausted we were when we got back that night.

Weird and wonderful machines appeared on the road at this period. Inventors flourished and in Melford we had our share of them. Mr. Yellowly, a retired gentleman who lived at Falkland House on the Green, made a four-wheeled pedal cycle. He arranged two large wheels on each side with a seat between the two. It was a big clumsy thing, but he managed to cycle as far as Cavendish on it. He also invented a flying machine, but he was not so successful with this. He built a platform in a tree in his garden, made wings and attached them to his arms, climbed up on to the platform and at a given signal the gardener had to pull a rope and release the platform. Down he came – crash – and that was the end of that experiment.

The next great change in our lives was the advent of the horseless carriage. The first cars I remember sounded like traction engines; they were very noisy and objectionable, and needed no warning horn to hear them coming. To comply with regulations, two able-bodied men had to be in charge of these mechanically propelled vehicles, and a third man had to walk in front with a red warning flag. Five miles an hour was considered a furious speed. A great advance was made when, in 1896, the law was changed and no longer demanded the use of the red flag, and the speed limit was raised to twelve miles per hour. Petrol was bought at the chemist at that time. In 1903 the speed limit was raised to twenty miles per hour, but no sensible person was ever expected to drive at such a rate.

The villagers looked on the cars with very mixed feelings. I heard that in one Suffolk village the people piled farm wagons on the road to stop them, but Melford took them more philosophically, though with much suspicion. The older men particularly disliked them and talk in the pubs was no longer about the rotation of the crops and kindred subjects, but these "'ere new-fangled morty cars".

"'Tis the invention of the devil."

"It 'ont last; it can't last; scares the 'osses out of their wits."

Some thought they were a mechanical toy to amuse the rich, and would die out in time. Many thought they were a public nuisance and motorists in general were dangerous lunatics.

These curious-looking inventions (and some of the early ones were indeed curious) would often be drawn up outside a pub and, as some proud owner tinkered with his new model trying to start it up, such remarks as the following would be heard:

"Ain't she bufull?"

"Don't think nawthen to it mesen."

"Must a corst a tidy bit."

"That 'ere sheen 'ont stut." (machine won't start)

And from the tone of his voice, he sincerely hoped his words would be proved correct.

As the smart carriages and broughams of the wealthy were gradually ousted by motor cars, coachmen, grooms and stable boys had to learn (often very reluctantly) to struggle with clutches and gears. Some of the older men, who had lived with horses all their lives, couldn't get out of the habit of shouting "Whoa!" Many were the noisy and hostile encounters on the roads. The horses were very frightened at the noisy contraptions they met, and there were quite a lot of accidents. As for the verbal encounters on the roads, these were highly inflammable, even to the point of blows.

One of the first cars in Melford was built by Mr. Medcalf. An occasion arose when I had to go to Cambridge on urgent business. Mr. Sewell, our manager, was very seriously ill and the only chance to save his life was for a specialist to operate on him without delay. There was no available telephone so Mr. Medcalf agreed to take me there. The journey took over four hours and the engine broke down three times. Going through Horseheath we met some horses from Newmarket with their trainer and a stable boy. The horses took fright at our noisy machine and unseated the boy. Fortunately he hung on to the horse or it would have bolted.

I managed to get to Cambridge in time to see the specialist and arrange with him to come over immediately to operate on Mr. Sewell. But he dared not risk coming back with us by car; instead he caught the last train back to Melford and was just in time to save Mr. Sewell's life. We had to stop in Cambridge for the night as we daren't try to go back at night. The next day we made the return journey without serious mishap, though we had to stop several times to make adjustments to the machinery. If Mr. Medcalf hadn't been such a skilled mechanic we should never have arrived at all.

Fred Sewell was a clever mechanic and never minded how long he spent on a job. One evening he was called out on some job just as he was about to close his shop in Hall Street, and he forgot to return. The next morning when he went to work the shop door was still open, the light on, and his day's takings of little piles of coins still on the counter as he had left it the night before.

Fred had one of the earliest cars and enjoyed telling of his exploits with it. He and some friends planned a day's outing to Clacton. All went well for a few miles until from the back seat came shouts:

"Whoa, Fred."

"What's up?"

"Car's afire."

Smoke was seeping through the floor board and they found the straw padding of the back seat was alight. They soon remedied that, and on they went. The engine stalled once or twice and at the mere suggestion of a hill they all got out and pushed. Just within sight of Clacton another shout from the back seat:

"Whoa, Fred."

"What's up?"

"Car's afire agin."

Out they all climbed and dealt with that. Coming home, the acetylene lights functioned only occasionally, but as they were travelling mostly through country lanes they didn't worry too much, till they suddenly realised they had lost their way.

"Never mind," said Fred (always an optimist). "We'll keep gooing. We'll get somewhere. The moon 'ull be up soon. That 'ull show us the direction."

Suddenly there was another diversion. Going through a village they saw in the light of an open door of a pub, two men in full evening dress and top hats. They staggered outside and started fighting, encouraged by cheering onlookers.

"We marn't miss this."

So they stopped the car and enjoyed the spectacle. In due course they got near home and, strange to relate, just as they reached the top of Ballingdon Hill their flickering lamp came on again and stayed alight sufficiently for them to reach home in safety. All agreed it was a "werry nice day's outing".

My first car was a second-hand Austin, number plate GV 3. I bought it from Miss Bull of Borley Rectory. It had a very good engine, and an umbrella-like collapsible roof so you could have it open or closed. I was tremendously proud of it until some irate driver of a large farm cart squeezed me into the high kerb on Sudbury Market Hill and shouted, "Get that bleeding perambulator out of the way." Come to think of it, it did look rather like a perambulator, but it served me well for many years.

Mr. Chinnery of Acton was the first bus proprietor to offer a regular passenger and carrier service. This was in 1919 and it ran from the Black Lion to Sudbury once a week. Later this was extended to a daily service and was always very reliable and very well patronised.

After a while Mr. Chinnery became more ambitious and started a daily bus service to London, and one day I decided to risk a journey. The bus had wooden sides and slatted seats and springs of doubtful efficiency. It was an exciting adventure and I enjoyed viewing the open countryside, but by the time I arrived in London I wondered why I had ever undertaken such a journey. I wriggled and twisted, first this way and that and couldn't find a comfortable spot anywhere. But I had to make the return journey, and by the time I got home every bone in my body ached.

Another early bus service I recollect was that run by the ex-sailor, Mr. Brown. His bus, too, was a primitive affair, with wooden sides and seats and small windows, somewhat like a box on wheels. He was a very obliging man and you could take all sorts of luggage on board – live hens if you wanted to. The door was rather low and he had the kindly habit of warning his lady passengers of the danger of this. Every time he stopped for a passenger to alight, he would call out, "Mind yer 'ead ladies, little low." This occurred so regularly that when he got as far as "Mind yer 'ead ladies" the passengers would chorus "little low."

18

FOOTBALL

There are records of a Football Club in Melford as far back as 1868. At that time a local butcher supplied animal bladders, which were covered with hessian, for footballs. These were very fragile and it was not unusual for two or three to burst during a game. Those wearing hobnail boots were not allowed to take part.

About the year 1885, Mr. Bernard Hurst, the organist, introduced more organised football, and in this he was assisted by Mr. George Leggatt of Sudbury, who coached the teams in the Football Association rules. My father was secretary of the club, and the rector, the Rev. C.J. Martyn, who was always a keen supporter and a good sportsman himself, allowed the club to use the rectory meadow for their games. For their away matches he lent them a pair of horses and his brake.

The rectory meadow was not exactly ideal as it was very sloping and at that time had a deep ditch from Kentwell, often filled with water, running through it. The goals consisted of two posts with a tape for cross-bars, so, as one can easily imagine, there were often arguments as to whether the ball went under or over the "bar". Goal nets hadn't been invented, and there were no lines or linesmen, only corner posts. Each team brought their own umpire in those days, and there were often fierce arguments between the umpires, the spectators joining in with great gusto. Free fights were not uncommon.

At first they played in their ordinary working clothes with red handkerchiefs tied round their necks, but later they adopted a uniform which consisted of a tam-o-shanter woollen cap with a tassel, thick buckskin trousers fastened below the knee with a large buckle, and heavy boots. But Mr. Hurst continued to wear long trousers long after the others had abandoned the custom – and he always wore his glasses too.

They played "friendly" matches against other villages, but as brute force was the order of the day it might almost be described as a battle rather than a sport. When losing, the captain would call his men together in the middle of the field. "Come on together," he'd say, and they'd charge down the field en masse with the ball straight into the goal. It was considered very bad sportsmanship to kick or trip a man and this was severely condemned. But hip and shoulder charging was allowed and this was done very effectively.

Bernard Hurst developed a particularly powerful charge, much to the surprise of many of his opponents, as he was a small, gentlemanly fellow. He was fond of telling how when he was living at Cavendish he introduced football to the village, and one day a would-be player, Harry Thompson, was sent flying by one of his powerful charges. On recovering himself Harry said, "Excuse me, Mr. Hurst, but is that football?"

"Yes Harry."

"Then I'll bid you good afternoon Mr. Hurst," and raising his cap he walked off the field.

When on the point of making a particularly heavy charge Bernard would run alongside a man, snatch off his cap, charge his opponent, then stand still and carefully replace his cap (and often his glasses) before resuming play.

My father too was a powerful man and his shoulder charges had a demoralising effect on his opponents. He took delight in shouldering them into the ditch and I've seen a man somersault twice and go straight into the water, completely disappearing for a few seconds. Father was very tricky on the field; he clowned a lot and this delighted the spectators. Trimmer Andrews was another colourful player. He was a small man, quiet and inoffensive, and a keen fisherman. But on the football field he looked a fierce fellow with his red handkerchief tied round his neck knotted at the corners. He was a real terror charging straight down the whole length of the field after the ball.

One day the rector, Rev. Martyn, who was a keen supporter of the club, arranged an outing for the team to see Preston North End (English Cup and League winners of that year) play Cambridge University. They were so impressed with the fine style of this northern team, and especially the passing and their clever tactics, that they decided to adopt this method. They did this with such success that the next season they won all their matches except one. And this one loss might be attributed to rather too long a stay at Maplestead Cock on their way to play Halstead, it being Boxing Day, and they being in a mood to celebrate.

Now that the Melfordians had gained such proficiency, they boldly wrote to Ipswich Town and challenged them to a friendly match, but they received a somewhat churlish reply, to the effect that it would lower the prestige of Ipswich to play "little village teams". So in the following season, 1887-8, they decided to enter for the Suffolk Senior Cup. They beat both Stowmarket and Beccles in the early rounds. Then they met

Ipswich Town in the semi-final, and beat them at Portman Road by two goals to one. A local newspaper carried the headline "What about the Little Village now?" – since when the Melford club has often been referred to as the Little Village.

Football Team which won the Suffolk Senior Cup 1887/8.
Back row: Trimmer Andrews, E. Ardley, A. Ardley, J.O. Steed, W. Perry, C. Joslin (umpire), L. Fisher. Seated: A. Hurst, B.H. Hurst, J. Ambrose, F. Hurst. Reclining: J. Ardley.
Photo by T. C. Partridge, Sudbury

The final was a tremendous struggle between Woodbridge and Melford. The villagers made the mistake of over-training before the match, running several miles each night for a week before. This on top of their normal work was too much. However they just managed to draw 2–2. In the return match the following Saturday, however, they won 1–0. Great were the rejoicings in Melford that night, with a torchlight procession and cheers and shouting all the way from the station to the Bull, their meeting place at the time. Their team had two sets of three brothers and consisted of B.H. Hurst (Captain), F. Hurst, A. Hurst, W. Perry, C. Andrews (Trimmer), A. Ardley, J. Ardley, E. Ardley, J.O. Steed, L.G. Fisher, and my father, J. Ambrose.

Quite a few well-known personalities played for the club in those early matches. There was William Neville Cobbold who played for England against Scotland, Ireland and Wales in 1883 and 1888. Another distinguished player, although he did not play very often, was H. Wickham Steed, editor of *The Times*, who was from a prominent Melford family. The colours black and white were chosen by Sir William Hyde Parker. He and his brother were players prior to 1885. They were in their House football team at Eton, whose colours these were, so they suggested them for Melford.

The season of 1894-5 was another great milestone in the club's history. Melford ran three elevens that year, all of them being very successful. By now the rector was the Rev. G. St. J. Topham and he was chairman of the club. This year the club again reached the final of the Suffolk Senior Cup by defeating Saxmundham 2-1. The news was brought to Melford by carrier pigeon. It was said that nearly 1,700 people gathered at the station to greet the heroes. The rector's brake was there to meet them with ropes attached and about thirty-odd men dragged the brake with the victors aboard up the street to the deafening cheers of the tremendous crowd, preceded by the Melford Brass Band playing "Here the Conquering Heroes come". Houses were decorated with flags and banners and many carried lighted torches.

With all these exciting things going on in the village it was no wonder all we schoolboys wanted to be footballers and play for the village team. The Green provided an excellent place for would-be champions to practise, and there was almost always a game or two going on there. We had no organised games at all at school, so we arranged our own, and even before I left school a group of us formed our own team. We used to walk to Sudbury on a Saturday afternoon and play against another team on People's Park. Then we'd visit Tommy Gates' little teashop in Station Road and have a penny cup of tea and a penny three-cornered jam tart – very tasty and nice – and then walk back home.

Whenever Melford played Sudbury at the Sudbury ground, we youngsters would always make a point of going to see the match. Well-to-do tradesmen of the district, including Mr. Whittle, stood together behind the goal posts at the Friars Street end, watching the game in a dignified manner, puffing big cigars. It was quite a pretty sight to see the smoke rising and we liked to get a whiff of the cigars and, if we got a chance, to listen to some of their caustic remarks on the play.

Round the rest of the ground the townspeople shouted and rang handbells, accompanied by bang...bang...bang on a corrugated iron fence along one side. Of course Sudbury and Melford were always strong rivals and there was almost always a shindy of some sort or other, and it was not at all unusual for a fight or two to break out between rival supporters before the day ended. On one occasion the Melford crowd was stoned along North Street by some roughs. I'm pretty sure though that Sudbury had a great respect for Melford. And Melford reckoned themselves a goal up when they walked on the ground!

When I was fifteen (in 1893) I was able to save up two shillings and sixpence and become a member of the Melford Football Club. For this you were issued with a smart fixture card and allowed into all home matches, and it also entitled you "to personally introduce a Lady Friend to the ground on the occasion of Home Matches free of charge". There were about eighty members of the club at this time.

In 1898 I was asked to be secretary, a job I did at various times over the years. One day in my capacity as secretary I received a telegram from W. Boggis (who was working in London) and who was due to play that day, to say he'd missed his train. I dashed along to the captain, Harry Steed, who was by now already changing for the match at his brother's house, and showed him the telegram.

"Well it's just time to start," he said. "You'll have to take his place.

"Phew no. I'm not even considered good enough for the reserves," I replied.

"Well I can't run about after anyone else now, so you'll just have to do what you can."

The match was against Sudbury of all teams. When I appeared on the ground the remarks I heard were far from complimentary. I was put at left half. Sudbury had a clever outside right named Du Pont. I made up my mind to shadow him throughout the game, and was able not only to frustrate him but actually managed to feed the forwards in front of me. The result of the game was a draw. When it was over I was proclaimed a minor hero and told I would be in the first team from then on.

At this time our formation was five forwards, three half backs and two full backs. Several of us worked at the Mat Factory and we often talked about football, planning our various methods of attack and defence. This was a great help and improved our combination.

In those days players paid for all their own kit but not their travelling expenses. For long-distance matches the club would hire a horse-drawn wagonette from the Bull, but when playing Sudbury they would think nothing of walking there and returning again on foot. They would strip off at the Angel and play on the town ground, amid cheers and jeers from the exuberant crowd. We had no training and often never touched a ball from one week to the next.

Sometimes a young player would be afraid to play because his parents were opposed to it, thinking he might get injured and be unable to go to work. We had no medical help or advice, and if a player did get hurt we did the best we could for him ourselves. One of our players, Button Cadge, broke his arm, and I can remember him sitting on the Hall Bridge, frightened to go home. No substitutes were allowed, so we were careful not to get hurt.

Once when playing Ipswich Town at Melford one of their forwards charged me and bowled me over. Later in the game I retaliated and charged him heavily. He came at me gesticulating furiously, and I responded in a wordy justification of my action. One of the Ipswich team laughed at me: "No use talking to him, old chap, he's deaf and dumb." In the dressing room we shook hands and after that were always the best of friends.

On another occasion we were visiting Cambridge to play a team which is now Cambridge United. This was a very rough match and we were pelted with stones and tufts of grass after the match. We had a couple of good boxers in our team. We all got together and challenged any Cambridge spectator to come and fight, one at a time. But we got no response.

We once had a visiting player, a Scotsman, who was a relative of Tipney Theobald. On this occasion we hired a brake to drive down to Sudbury to play but he refused to ride with us, saying he preferred to run there. He ran the whole way to Sudbury alongside our brake, played an excellent game, then ran all the way back. He certainly was a tough one.

One Saturday, just before Christmas Day, we had to play Haverhill. Unfortunately our train got in two hours before the match was due to begin. Some of the players, feeling merry and bright, spent the time imbibing non too wisely. In the first half Haverhill scored four goals. At the beginning of the second half one of our merry players, who had already been cautioned, was turned off by the referee. Another player, his cousin, went up to the referee and asked "if he'd got a bob on the game". He too was promptly turned off. This infuriated us, but also sobered us up, and with only nine men we saw Haverhill scored no more goals. The two that were sent off went up the town in a gay mood, and when we caught up with them they were giving a lecture on the greatness of Melford Football Club outside a butcher's shop.

"First we had a rag ball; then we had a tennis ball; then we got a proper ball, and now see what we've done."

The butcher came out sharpening his knife and muttering, "I'll make some on 'em pay for this tonight."

Apparently he'd made a bet on the game and lost.

A party of keen Melford supporters went to watch our team play at Bury. After the match they went to the Castle to have a drink, the landlord being a Melford man, Jimmy Dutton. They enjoyed themselves so much that they missed the last train back to Melford, so they started walking home. At Sicklesmere they took the first turning to the left instead of the second, and after walking six miles found themselves in Felsham. But they were highly delighted to find they had arrived about half an hour before closing time, so they consoled themselves in the warm and friendly hostelry before starting off again on their way back to Melford. They arrived about three in the morning, having walked an extra six miles out of their way.

The club had much difficulty in finding a suitable ground and made many moves before finally coming to rest at Stoneylands. But in spite of these difficulties they continued to do well. I was a member of the team which scored the third Suffolk Senior Cup victory in 1908-9 which at that time put an end to Ipswich Town's run of success of five years. In the final we beat Bury at Portman Road, Ipswich, by an only goal scored by Tom Wickham, a clever player. David Border was captain of our team that year.

I went on playing for the club for over twenty years, until I was forty-two years old. During that time I acted as secretary and captain at various times. Since that time, after many vicissitudes, Melford has won the Suffolk Senior Cup seven times in all, their most notable period of success being in 1952-3, 1953-4 and 1954-5. I think it will be many years before such a record is again achieved by a Suffolk village.

19

Shepherd's Friendly Society

On Christmas Day in 1826 a few friends were gathered together at the Friendship Inn at Ashton-under-Lyne, Lancashire, celebrating the occasion and enjoying themselves. Because they were having such a happy time together they felt they would like to do something to help others for whom life was more difficult, especially those who were unable to work because of ill health and sickness. So they decided to form a Friendly Society. As there were twelve of them present and it was Christmas time, they said they'd like to call their society the Shepherds after the Good Shepherd. The Society expanded rapidly and scores of lodges sprang up all over the United Kingdom and in the colonies. A lodge was formed in Melford in 1873.

My mother enrolled me in the juvenile section when I was seven years old and I have been a member ever since. The first secretary of the Melford Lodge was Mr. Butcher, then Chas. Spilling, followed by George Reynolds. The manager of the Mat Factory, Mr. Chas. Sewell, used to help Mr. Reynolds by drawing up the annual balance sheet, and it was here that I became interested in the work of the society, and felt that it was a very worthwhile service to working people, as of course there was no such thing as a national sickness benefit at that time.

By 1909 I had progressed so well at the office that I was now earning twenty-five shillings a week, a good wage in those days. Indeed I felt so well-established that I decided I could afford to get married, and in September of that year I married Miss Kate Sewell, daughter of our manager. Mr. Canham of Ipswich, who was a great friend of the governor Mr. Whittle, lent us his brougham and a fine pair of horses for the occasion, as a wedding present. It was a splendid turn-out, and for this auspicious occasion I even bought myself a top hat.

But back to the Shepherds. I took over the secretaryship in 1913, the year the Friendly Societies were merged into the state scheme. The Friendly Societies played a very important part in the early stages of the national health service. That year I attended an A.M.C. (Annual Moveable Conference) for the first time. To me it was a most impressive and interesting experience, coming as I did from a small country village. It was held at Stoke-on-Trent and the proceedings were carried out with much pomp and ceremony. The speeches were fiery and impressive, full of great rhetoric and high-sounding ideals, though perhaps not always very grammatically expressed. To me it was a marvellous thing to belong to such a grand organisation doing such wonderful work for the ordinary working people. I was lucky enough to be accommodated at one of the best hotels in the town. This too impressed me greatly as I had not experienced such luxury before.

As time went on I represented our district at many A.M.C.s and have been received by provosts at Glasgow, Edinburgh, Dundee and Aberdeen, and mayors in several towns in England. I usually played the organ for the opening and closing ceremonies. I found the Scots particularly witty and entertaining. After the weighty discussions at their meetings during the day, they would relax in the evenings and play all sorts of schoolboyish jokes on one another, just as we did in Melford.

On one occasion they transferred a W.C. notice from a lavatory to the door of a friend who had retired early. Then they sat in the lounge watching the comings and goings. They were pastmasters at contriving jokes on their pals. I remember one old gentleman, a very aged one, who regularly attended A.M.C.s, always refused to go by an express train. He said it was too dangerous, so he chose instead to go by a train that stopped at every station.

Some of the early pioneers in the Melford Lodge were rare characters. Though they may not have been highly educated, they were very sound in their judgments and took the work of the society seriously and conscientiously. Consequently it flourished and with their careful management built up a sound financial position, even though one or two of them, when studying the balance sheet, used to say "I can't make nawthin' out o' this 'ere balance sheet. The figures are the same both sides."

In the early days the subscriptions were very small. The sick pay too was not much, but it was a big help where there was a family to support, and members soon became aware of the wisdom of belonging to such a society. Sick visitors were appointed and they took their work very seriously. They would walk miles to visit a sick member of the club to make sure he was genuine. Woe betide him if he was found carrying a pail of water or digging a root of potatoes in his garden. He would be reported and duly dealt with. But there was precious little absenteeism in the early days – men couldn't afford to be off work, in fact they went on working many a time when they should not have done so.

When the national health scheme came in it considerably altered the situation. Men found it difficult to pay the subscriptions for the friendly society and also for the state scheme, the average wage at that time being about fifteen shillings. But those who did keep up their subscriptions became eligible for two lots of sick pay when ill – twelve shillings from the club and ten shillings from the state. When this became apparent there were a good many more members staying on the club for longer periods – it was a tempting situation – and we had to tighten our rules.

Lodge nights were held once a month at our room at the Black Lion. On these nights members paid their dues for the month. We usually got our business finished about ten o'clock. The pub would be open till eleven at this time (when the Liberals came into power they reduced the opening hours in an endeavour to reduce excessive drinking). Having completed our business upstairs we would descend to the smoke room, where we would pass round the hat and everyone would contribute a penny or two for the beer. We'd get a gallon or more, and one man would appoint himself pourer. Then someone would call for a song. At first the answer would be "Ah no, I can't," but as the beer flowed more freely, everyone wanted to sing.

All sorts of humorous country songs were sung. One man's speciality was about Sarah Bailey, who had a wooden leg. The singer would use his stick to bang on the floor at the appropriate moment. There were lots of verses and the chorus went like this:

And her leg went down with a dot and carry one,
As she stomped along so gaily.

There's many a worse gal, though she's sere upon the pins
Is me lovely Sarie Bailey.

The assembled company would join in and bang vigorously as "the leg went down". It was good fun and we all enjoyed ourselves.

We used to have annual dinners, which were always sumptuous and hilarious affairs. These were held at the Black Lion and a typical menu would be:

1st course: Huge joints of roast and boiled beef; roast and boiled mutton, with plenty of root vegetables.
2nd course: Chicken with roast potatoes and green vegetables.
3rd course: Plum pudding and various pies.
4th course: Bread or biscuits and cheese.

The big joints of meat would be carved at the table by officials who presided at each table. We'd drink a loyal toast, and from then on beer would flow pretty freely. It was supplied free at first, after that it had to be paid for. It was mostly draught beer but a special treat would be a bottle of Bass at fourpence. It was considered a luxury and we thought it better than wine. Finally such remarks would be heard as "Ah, a werry good meal." "Ah fare full."

Of course we had to have a bit of business; a few reports and comments from the chairman and secretary, but by this time speech had often become a little confused and blurred. However the assembled company were equally mellow and ready to applaud the most modest effort at speech-making. Then came the jollifications, all free and easy, puffing at clay pipes, calling for ale. I was usually pressed into service on the piano. Invariably the poacher's song was called for, and with loud voices and complete abandon we sang:

> I love me wife, me pipe and me glass,
> Gaily along thro' life's journey I pass;
> Jolly and free, it just suits me,
> Up with me gun in the mornin'.

There were dozens of verses, altered to suit any current event, but everyone joined in the chorus, banging their tankards on the bare tables. Other popular songs were "Simon the cellarer keeps a rare store" and "Little brown jug", and I remember one particularly hilarious occasion when Jim Hostler, a local comic singer, came as a visitor. He placed himself in such a position beside the pianist that he was standing just behind a gentleman with a bald head, and the chorus of his song went:

> He tickled; I tickled; he giggled; I giggled;
> The more he giggled the more I tickled;
> And he said to me –
> Don't you be ridicu–lus
> Don't you come and tickle us –
> Go and tickle someone else,
> But don't tickle me.

As he sang the song he made pretence to tickle the top of the old man's bald head. The old boy was quite oblivious of this action but he laughed as much as the others. It was an uproarious occasion.

Sometimes we had a more serious or sentimental song. On

one occasion Paddy Lambert of Lyston Hall was our guest for the evening. A pathetic song was sung by Sam Ford, describing the sorrows of an old couple who had to live separately in the workhouse: "Was it right to part this dear old man and wife?" Mr. Lambert, who was a very kind-hearted man, was really upset by this and said he never realised that this was the policy of workhouses, and declared he would enquire into the matter. He was a member of the Board of Guardians and in this capacity he was able to get the rules altered so that life was made easier for married couples at Walnuttree.

We had some very enjoyable district meetings. When I first joined our District H.Q. was at Bardfield and to get there I'd take a train to Haverhill, and from the Bell Hotel would hire a pony and trap and drive the rest of the way. It was a lovely outing in summer months. We met at the house of the district secretary, Mr. Charley Piper, a real old-fashioned gentleman with a long beard.

Another colourful character was Oscar Mayes, a farmer who lived at Felsham. We used to drive over there and audit his accounts. He brewed some of the most beautiful beer I've ever tasted and he'd always give us a glass to fortify ourselves before starting on the accounts. He was a great hand at telling humorous stories of his young days. He once spent a jolly evening at Sudbury and returned home having taken on more than a few whiskies. On arrival at Felsham he went outside and was gone so long that his family went out to look for him. They found him undressing and climbing into the haystack, which he declared was his bed.

Another Friendly Society, the Buffalos, which functioned in Melford, invited some of us to a sausage supper at the gamekeeper's cottage at Kentwell. Eight of us went and we had a grand time. We came out of the cottage at one in the morning and zigzagged down the avenue. We managed to push each other over the stile, when suddenly someone called out, "We ain't all 'ere."

We counted and found Darkie was missing.

"'E may 'ave fallen into the moat," we decided, so back we all went to look for him. We found him sleeping peacefully in a ditch and it seemed a pity to disturb him. At this point we got confused as to which way to turn, and somehow or other Charlie Bixby and I got separated from the rest. The next thing I remember was when the butler from Kentwell came out and said, "Come on in you chaps, and have a bottle of champagne with me." I regret to say we accepted his invitation. I still can't remember how we got home that night.

When a death occurred of one of our members the society would supply bearers to carry the coffin. If the death happened to be on the outskirts of the village as many as six bearers would be needed, and sometimes two extra ones would attend to change over from time to time. They used to cover the coffin and the heads of the bearers (except the two who walked in front) with a heavy black velvet pall. On a hot day and for a long journey this was quite an ordeal. As secretary I would walk in front with the chairman. We had special black and silver funeral sashes and carried silver crooks. One of us would deliver a special oration at the graveside.

20

Volunteers and Territorials

I had been working at the Mat Factory for about two years when I heard that Mr. Whittle had invited the Volunteers to his home at Babergh Hall for manoeuvres. Knowing I was interested he invited me to go and watch. The Melford Company defended the Hall and the Sudbury Company marched in and attacked. After this great battle, in which there were no casualties, the officers were invited into the Hall for dinner, while the rank and file were regaled outside with two large barrels of strong beer and pork pies. I was a spectator. After dinner Mr. Whittle came out, and seeing me said, "Go in and help yourself."

I found myself alone in the dining room. There upon the long table were the remains of the most delicious food and the widest variety of drinks I had ever seen, all of the best quality. I sampled here and there, and more and more. "Phew, that tastes good. I'll have just a little drop more." Having had my fill I went outside. When I got into the fresh air again I suddenly realised what had happened to me, and decided I had better make tracks for home as quickly as I could. The long road seemed to be coming up to meet me, and I had a rare job to get home.

It was reported afterwards (and talked about for many a

day) that I wasn't the only one who had dined unwisely. Even the officers, when they came outside, drew their swords and offered to fight duels with all and sundry; the men too, under the influence of the strong ale, had a rare problem to form fours when the order was given. They staggered about forming threes and fives. It was decided to have rifle inspection and orders were given for blank ammunition to be handed in. But even after this, on the march home, a rifle went off now and then.

The march back to Melford and Sudbury was by all accounts a comical sight, with the men and officers too rolling along the road, but it succeeded without undue casualties apart from a few who fell by the roadside. The result of the exercise was summed up thus: "The attack was werry good – but the defence was ty-rific."

This, my first insight into volunteer army life, in no way dismayed me, and when I was fifteen in 1893 I joined the Volunteers, though I was under age. I found the training very varied and useful, and as time went on it became more and more interesting. After a while I was able to go to training camp occasionally and this was a new experience for me. These were weekend camps and we all enjoyed them. It made a nice break from work and was the nearest we got to a holiday. Grey and red uniforms were supplied as well as boots, so there was always a chance of getting a new pair of boots if you went to camp. And I might mention there were always a tidy few among our company on the lookout for such items. Rations were supplied as well, and it was noticed that though some of the Melford men went to camp with empty haversacks, they were bulging on their return journeys.

I'm afraid some of the Melford company had a reputation for being on the make-haste, but they were a grand crowd of men and we thoroughly enjoyed these camps, where there was always a great deal of banter and good humour. No problem ever stumped the Melford Company; they were master men for improvisation and never got stuck for anything.

Melford Old Volunteers, c. 1906. Cyclists' Section outside Lecture Hall. Left to right: Sgt. Higginson, E. Ambrose, W. Sewell, G.H. Bell, — Maxin, — Fisk, — Weldon, — Deakin.
Photo by E. Ambrose

Early on I was transferred to the Cyclists Corps and when in camp we used to patrol the coasts in the area of Yarmouth and Lowestoft. It was terribly hard-going as the roads were still very bad at that time. After a while I reached the rank of sergeant. When the Boer War broke out in 1899 each company was asked to send one volunteer. Bert Perkins went as representative of the Melford Company.

In 1907 the Old Volunteers were merged into the Territorials, and after that we had opportunities to attend camps for a week at Colchester, Aldershot and other military barracks. I can recollect when we were at Aldershot we had manoeuvres (this was just before 1914) in the Long Valley, and at the same time the regulars too were having manoeuvres. I was very impressed with the physique and efficiency of this fine body of men; they looked fit for anything. They later became known as the Old Contemptibles and their strength was proved in the early stages of the 1914-18 war.

As the prospect of a war became more imminent, we were told to keep our bags packed in readiness. I remember clearly the night before mobilisation. We had had a special choir practice at the church as we were going to sing for Mr. Hurst's daughter's wedding the next day. We practised a special chant which I had composed. After leaving the church I walked down the casey and met a friend outside the school and we talked about the possibility of war. The sky was blood red; was this an omen, we wondered?

By post next morning I received my calling-up paper with notice to report at the Drill Hall at Sudbury at one in the afternoon. We had to leave everything (my plans to play at the wedding; my account books at work which I had left unbalanced – and I still dream about this at times) – and go off and play our part in the war.

We turned up at the Drill Hall in full strength; not a man was missing out of the whole battalion of nearly a thousand men formed from companies in towns and villages in our area. We had medical inspection and of course several were pronounced unfit. We had to march down from the Drill Hall to Sudbury Station, and those who had been turned down on medical grounds marched alongside us, some with tears in their eyes, they were so disappointed. Many of these men, after having much needed medical attention, turned up afterwards and joined their companies.

When we mobilised the regular instructors made us as efficient as part-time soldiers could be expected to be. Our NCOs were a great help in training recruits. It was decided to form a 2nd and 3rd/ 5th Battalion Suffolks, and I was transferred to staff to help form these companies. Our training continued and we produced some of the toughest and fittest of men. Before long new battalions were formed and sent to France, where we were attached to other regiments. The Suffolks played a gallant part in the war.

I served with them for four years, the last two in France. When I was finally demobilised and returned to England I found a great change in the country; there was a spirit of discontent and disillusionment. Even in our own much-loved little village, life was never the same again.

*

When I look back over my ninety-four years of life it seems utterly incredible to realise the vast changes which have taken place.

When I was a child the roads and footpaths were used for man to walk along, and we shared them leisurely with the animals. There was no need for pavements to separate man from beast. Now man requires special protection, and one needs to keep alert to stay alive!

It was a job requiring considerable effort for my grandmother to prepare a cup of tea; to get sticks dry enough to catch light with the help of a tinderbox; to coax them carefully till sufficient heat was generated; to pump water from the well and patiently await boiling point. At times it still seems incredible to me that at the touch of a switch, electric power will do all this in a matter of minutes.

When I was small it created great excitement if a horse bolted, and considered quite an important item of news if someone fell out of their wagon in our own or a neighbouring village. Wars were only vaguely heard of in far away foreign parts, not having anything to do with our peaceful way of life. But now at the touch of another switch radio and TV gives us full and instantaneous details of events from every part of the world. I still find this difficult to appreciate at times. The rapid march of science and technology goes on apace and fresh discoveries are made beyond our wildest dreams – on into the nuclear age and now into the space age. I often wonder: is there still more to come, or are we reaching a climax?

With all these thoughts in mind my wife and I decided it would be interesting and enjoyable to make this record of how these changes came to our little corner of England, just in case some future generation may care to learn what life was like when I was young, ninety-four years ago.

Local Words, Common Expressions and Pronunciations

Appletite = Appetite
A-stiddy = Instead of
Axe = Ask (Axe me ass = Ask my donkey = Ask a silly question)
Back'us = Back house or wash house
Bettying/Bopping = Bobbing up and down
Bor = Boy
Buss = Embrace
Cail = To stone (Cailed 'em up the street = stoned them up the
    street)
Clane = Clean
Clapt eyes on = Saw
Clars = Claws (Hands)
Claw 'old on = Catch hold of
Coom = Come
Coterage = Small cottage
Crop = Throat (Stuck in me crop)
Curchy = Curtsey
Dannick = Little bread roll
Dawzled = Dazed; half stupefied
Decatedly = Decidedly
Dicky = Shirt front, also Feeling unwell
Dosselled = Dazzled

189

Dreffle = Dreadful
Durg = Animal droppings = dung
Enow = Enough
Extry = Extra
Fare = Quite; Seems (I fare full; that do fare strange)
Frawn = Frozen (A'm frawn a cold = frozen with cold)
Frowsy = Slovenly
Gaze = Picture
Greash = Grease
Haps or Happen = Perhaps
Harnser = Heron
Hazelled = Half dried (referring to washing)
Haysel = Haymaking time
Hingle = Hinge
Homedod or Hoddermedod = Snail
Hooker = Shepherd
Hoss = Horse
Hoom = Home
Impechivous = Impetuous
Jannicking (or Nanniking) = Fooling about; getting in the way
Jar = Jaw
Jelly = Toad
Jowned = Joined
Ketch = Catch (Ketch 'old 'on = Catch hold of)
Kiddler = Muddler
Laten = Brass
Looker = Overseer
Marn't = Must not
Mawther = Girl or woman
Missamedods = Midsummer bugs found under dry manure
Nawthen = Nothing

Oncommon = Uncommon
Oothum = With him
Peggles = Cowslips
Petty = Temper
Prinking = Making oneself smart
Pullicking = Complaining
Rafty = Raw cold
Rainy bug = Ladybird
Rennie = Small field mouse
Rick = Reach
Riddy on = Rid of
Roudle = Whisky flavoured water
Seal of the day = Greeting – good morning
Sheen = Machine
Siggify = Signify
Sole = Heavy blow (verb and noun)
Snew = Snowed
Spidgick = Sparrow
Spike = Workhouse
Sway = Decision ('e don't care the sway = influence a decision)
Tidy = Quite (a tidy few; tidy bit)
Tiffling = Pottering
Tipney Tauter or Titter me Tauter = See-saw
Tissick = Irritating cough
Trav'us = Blacksmith's forge (usually attached to house)
Urchin = Hedgehog
Valeration = Valuation
Wash'us = wash house
Went = Gone ('e shouldn't a went)
Werry= Very
Wholly = Fully

Wittles = Victuals
Woodly = Thick-headed (as with a stuffy head cold)
Worch = Throbbing pain

Ernest Ambrose was born in Long Melford, Suffolk in 1878, the son of a foreman at the local coconut matting factory. He was educated locally, and started work as a clerk in the same factory in 1890.

He served with the Suffolk Regiment during the First World War and, on demobilisation, became clerk in a local solicitor's office. He later became a housing manager for Melford Rural District Council. In 1938 he also became clerk to Long Melford parish council. He ran a general store in the village from 1950 until his retirement in 1967.

He was secretary and captain of the local football club, served with the Territorial Army for 24 years, was a keen bell-ringer for 78 years and an enthusiastic photographer for 50 years. He was also church organist from 1897 to 1944 in the neighbouring villages of Borley, Glemsford and Clare and was a founder of the Working Men's Club and British Legion in Long Melford.

He married his first wife, Kate, in 1910; she died in 1948. In 1950, he married his second wife, Emily, and moved to the nearby town of Sudbury.

His vivid, witty memories of nineteenth- and early twentieth-century rural life were originally published in 1972, in Ernest's 95th year. He died in 1973, and is buried in the graveyard at Holy Trinity Church, Long Melford.